Disordered Thought and Development

The Vulnerable Child: Studies in Social Issues and Child Psychoanalysis

Series Editors:
M. Hossein Etezady and Mary Davis

The Vulnerable Child series is based on work that comes out of an ongoing Vulnerable Child Study Group, founded by Theodore Cohen, MD. It is sponsored by the American Psychoanalytic Association, and in the past was co-sponsored by the Association for Child Psychoanalysis. For many years the group has met regularly to discuss what life events render children more vulnerable to developmental and emotional disturbances, and what interventions help to reduce that vulnerability. The study group presents a workshop looking at various aspects of these issues at the meetings of the American Psychoanalytic Association. Co-chairs of the study group are M. Hossein Etezady, MD, and Mary Davis, MD; Dr. Cohen remains involved as Chair Emeritus.

The Vulnerable Child series publishes volumes which arise from the work of the Study Group, and looks toward expanding offerings to other publications that address the issues which make children more vulnerable to mental health problems, as well as interventions that help to ameliorate that vulnerability.

Titles in the Series

Vulnerable Child Volume 1 edited by Bernard Pacella, Theodore B. Cohen, and M. Hossein Etezady
Vulnerable Child Volume 2 edited by Bernard Pacella, Theodore B. Cohen, and M. Hossein Etezady
Vulnerable Child Volume 3 edited by Bernard Pacella, Theodore B. Cohen, and M. Hossein Etezady
Clinical Perspectives on Reflective Parenting: Keeping the Child's Mind in Mind edited by M. Hossein Etezady and Mary Davis
Mothering without a Home: Attachment Representations and Behaviors of Homeless Mothers and Children by Ann Smolen with Alexandra Harrison
Disordered Thought and Development: Chaos to Organization in the Moment by Theodore Fallon with Susan P. Sherkow

Disordered Thought and Development

Chaos to Organization in the Moment

Theodore Fallon, Jr.
with Susan P. Sherkow

JASON ARONSON
Lanham • Boulder • New York • Toronto • Plymouth, UK

Published by Jason Aronson
A wholly owned subsidiary of Rowman & Littlefield
4501 Forbes Boulevard, Suite 200, Lanham, Maryland 20706
www.rowman.com

10 Thornbury Road, Plymouth PL6 7PP, United Kingdom

British Library Cataloguing in Publication Information Available

Library of Congress Cataloging-in-Publication Data

Fallon, Theodore, 1954- author.
Disordered thought and development : chaos to organization in the moment / Theodore Fallon ; with Susan P. Sherkow.
p. cm.
Includes bibliographical references and index.
ISBN 978-0-7657-1017-8 (cloth : alk. paper) -- ISBN 978-0-7657-1018-5 (electronic)
1. Child development deviations. 2. Developmentally disabled children--Services for. 3. Developmentally disabled children--Family relationships. 4. Pediatric neuropsychiatry. I. Sherkow, Susan P., 1944- author. II. Title.
RJ135.F35 2014
618.92'8--dc23

2013042482

∞ ™ The paper used in this publication meets the minimum requirements of American National Standard for Information Sciences Permanence of Paper for Printed Library Materials, ANSI/NISO Z39.48-1992.

Printed in the United States of America

Contents

Foreword

M. Hossein Etezady

The rapid accumulation of new findings in the expanding fields of neuroscience and molecular biology has greatly contributed to the gradual filling of gaps in our appreciation and understanding of the mind and the various aspects of emotional and cognitive functions in the course of development. This has provided us with new means and methods of objectification and quantification in many areas of particular interest from a psychoanalytic perspective. Examples among many such areas might be mentalization, theory of mind, thought process, organization of thought and memory and, more specifically, the role of affects and their signal function in defense, in conflict resolution and in compromise formation. Another major area thus made available for examination and exploration is the interface between the experiential/subjective and representational/interactive, on one hand, and their corresponding organic/physiological substrates on the other hand. This interface is where we might look for answers to questions regarding the nature and machinations of the magical mystery that bridges the soma to the psyche and the brain to the mind.

In considering subjective states as the main domain of psychoanalysis, we find that they are capable of being directly accessed only by the individual subject alone. Others can only perceive this indirectly, in verbal narrative, via identification or empathy, for example, in part or parts, or may or may not recognize, affirm, repudiate, mirror, negate or elaborate them, in some or all aspects. Since the essential subject of psychoanalysis is subjectivity itself, directly accessible only to that individual alone, we can rely on neuroscience to inform us about the elemental ingredients that constitute the concretely objective grounding that a balanced view of any state of mind would require. Interactions, whether viewed developmentally, casually in mundane daily dealings or therapeutically as in clinical encounters, occur in an inter-subjective field which is experienced differently by each side, and even so in areas of shared subjectivity and overlapping saliency. This difference is particularly informative with regard to attachment types as well as modes and states of relatedness that each side may be capable of engaging.

States of relatedness can be distinguished by their developmental levels and functional relevancy in three organizational modes: 1. the monadic mode (oral/primary narcissism/autoerotic), 2. the dyadic mode (transitional/anal-sadistic), and 3. the triadic mode (oedipal/normal-neurotic). A triadic state of relatedness implies satisfactory oedipal resolution of the infantile neurosis, sufficiently demarcated id, ego, superego boundaries as well as predominance of reality principle and secondary process over primary process thinking. The capacity to be alone in the presence of another emerges by the end of the first year, coinciding with the "dawning of inter-subjectivity." With the advent of rapprochement at about the middle until the end of the second year both the mother and the child face the challenge of learning to be in the presence of another, in a new way, as infantile omnipotence begins to recede and a post ambivalent stage is entered.

The transition from a dyadic state of relatedness to one that is triadic occurs hand in hand with establishing the beginnings of the capacity for self and object constancy (by end of the 3rd year), which itself is reliant on the optimal resolution of rapprochement. The so-called critical sub-phase of rapprochement coincides with the latter half of the second year. Optimal resolution of rapprochement is considered to be critical for the "healing of the split," to come about incrementally during one year of consolidation, from about ages 2 to 3, characterized by battles of will, often referred to as the terrible two's. By the end of the third year we should normally be able to see the germinating beginnings and gradual emergence of self and object constancy, tolerance of ambivalence as well as the capacity for self and interactive regulation guided by signal affects. By about age 4, having established the beginnings of self and object constancy, a triadic state of relatedness in the context of an oedipal organization can now be entered. By this time symbolic representation, the pretend mode of thinking, as well as language and narrative formation are beginning to be more reliably available.

"The three calamities of childhood," namely fear of loss of the object initially, followed by the fear of the loss of the love of the object and finally, fear of punishment represented by castration anxiety, may now be regulated by the use of signal-affects, in the service of the homeostatic function of the ego, maintaining narcissistic equilibrium as well as fine tuning self and interactive regulation. This, at this time, is best accomplished mainly by using defensive repression, as the oedipal resolution of the infantile neurosis begins to take hold. Repression thus fuels ego growth by diverting neutralized libidinal and aggressive energies into sublimated channels of discharge and adaptive aims, which allows the ego and its resources to grow, leading to increasing autonomy of the superego and the ego-ideal. Individuals may be fixated at, or regress to earlier levels of libidinal or ego development, archaic object relations, infantile omnipotence and grandiosity characteristic of pre-oedipal modes of relatedness. Fixations are more common in organic entities while regression is usually associated with psychological conditions or organic pathology arriving later in life.

Engagement in a triadic state of relatedness presents an oedipal constellation with new challenges that may be insurmountable for those who are vulnerable or at risk, due to nature, nurture or both. In an inter-subjective view, when we consider development, parenting, interactive regulation or relationships either in daily life or in the course of analytic treatment, levels of organization and modes as well as states of relatedness matter with similar importance on both sides of the intersubjective field.

In dealing with the subject of thought disorder and in order to better understand our patient's needs and experiences, or to identify needed interventions and formulate the therapist's part during treatment, insights provided by an ego-psychological conceptual model can be uniquely illuminating. Hartmann's meta-psychology of psychosis is based on the ego's lack of capability to neutralize primitive aggressive energy. Un-neutralized, aggression can overwhelm existing structures and derail developmental organization. Neutralization of aggression in this frame is originally provided via the mother's function as an auxiliary ego, while she strives to libidinize the interactive experience. Neutralization, or the fusion of aggressive and libidinal drives, crucially dependent upon caregivers' libidinal constancy and empathic resonance, provides the developing ego with a sustainable reservoir of fuel for self-re-enforcing activity, growth and adaptation. In cases of psychosis we encounter a predominance of primary process thinking and primary narcissism, insufficient self and object differentiation, diffuse ego boundaries, impaired reality processing and blurring of wish and thought with reality and action. Reality becomes intolerable unless broken down or distorted to fit in with the delusional reconstitution of an inner world which consists of archaic introjects and narcissistic part-objects. Briefly put, any factor interfering with the capacity of the ego to sufficiently neutralize aggressive energy in order to fuel progressive development and to establish organizational mastery at various levels of development, in susceptible individuals may produce psychosis. Such a pathogenic causation may be found anywhere from the molecular, organic and genetic levels to acquired vulnerability, whether internal or external, transient or permanent, at any developmental level and in any part of the life cycle. Risk and vulnerability take many shapes and run deep and far, both on the side of the innate givens, temperament and genetics as well as on the side of the facilitating environment, for example, concerning the quality and adequacy of the care and sometimes the fit between the particular child and the primary caregiver.

The Vulnerable Child Discussion Group #30 of the American Psychoanalytic Association, June 2012 in Chicago, titled "Psychoanalytic Perspective on Thought Disorder," has here been expanded to furnish the material for this volume. In his presentation, Theodore Fallon, on that occasion, featured organizational mastery as a super-ordinate requirement for progressive development. Expanding on his presentation in the present volume, he delves deeply into the intuitive and empathic capabilities that this kind of clinical encounter calls for and the challenges it presents. We can witness the chaos and disintegration that he describes and how holding, containing, mirroring, reflecting, meaning-making and libidinal constancy can cultivate affect tolerance and modulation, enhance self-cohesion, enrich structure formation and prepare the ground for the appearance of relative organizational mastery at each developmental level.

Susan Sherkow, in her response, uses her own experience in particular instances of patients presenting with a thought disorder. She addresses clinical questions within her own experience and on many levels of discourse in psychoanalytic as well as phenomenological terms. In the present volume the reader will find presented what is basic and well established in relation to, and in the light of the new and current knowledge, so that a rounder sense of understanding might be integrated as an aspect of the clinician's overall perspective. No less importantly yet more vividly however, one will find many samples of personal accounts of what psychoanalysis, and these child analysts in particular, can and try to do for this sector of our patient population and for their families, both for the immediate as well as their long-term needs, including those with irreversible and organically caused conditions.

At the dawn of the most exciting period of human history, thanks to our burgeoning information technology, we are now in the lofty position of being able to bring together multiple views and countless layers of complicated matter, along many independent dimensions, on a very large scale, or in fragments and minutia, either in concert or individually. For psychoanalysis and for the child analyst, immersion in the multi-faceted convergence of new facts and collection of fresh findings in neuro-behavioral and cognitive fields is the royal road to integration, where true appreciation of the centrality of organizational mastery, as a super-ordinate developmental line, may be reached. This volume aspires to contribute to the vast subject of thought disorders through such an attempt, in the direction of such integration, recognizing that what we know now will soon be dwarfed by the great insights still awaiting us in a not-so-distant future. The best is yet to come, as it has been said, and there is much to be learned, as we persevere in seeking answers to pressing questions asked today and to those we have not yet thought to ask.

—M. Hossein Etezady

Introduction

The original spark of this monograph began as a presentation about successful psychoanalytic work with psychotic adolescents. As I immersed myself in trying to understand what I had been doing with these psychotic adolescents, I began to see a process that underlay all of psychoanalytic work, and not just psychoanalytic work, but all development. The process envisioned underlay basic development and maturation of the mind.

As I see it now, it is the *process of maturation when a mind moves from one developmental level to the next*. In that process the mind reorganizes itself. Although that sounds simple enough, the puzzle is this: The mind as the object must be disorganized before it can be reorganized. Yet the mind itself as the agent of the organization is doing the organizing. How can the mind as the agent organize while the same mind as the object is disorganized?

Imagine a map that has been useful, but suddenly you discover that there are parts of the territory previously unknown. In order to assemble a new more useful map, you have to disassemble the old map and put the pieces you know together in relation to the newly discovered pieces. While you are doing that, however, there will be uncertainty about where you are actually going when you try to use the partly dissembled and partly reassembled map.

This is true for development. *The mind organizes what it knows of the world* with all the elements it knows positioned in relation to all the other elements. *When new elements, understandings or relationships between the elements are discovered, as a matter of course, the mind reorganizes its model of the world.* This process becomes particularly messy when you consider that one's model of the world includes oneself and one's own mind.

Consider the pre-oedipal child who suddenly realizes that in addition to having a relationship with her mother and her father, there is also a relationship between her mother and her father that does not include her. Suddenly she recognizes that her pre-oedipal model of the universe is limited. With time and effort, she re-organizes her model to match what she now understands to be true of the world, including her place in it.

The moments between recognizing the limited nature of an earlier model and having in mind a new model are filled with uncertainty, as there is neither an old model nor a new model to guide thoughts and actions. In these *moments* of uncertainty, there will be much anxiety and frustration until one settles on and emotionally invests in a more reliable new model. Take a moment to again consider the state of a child in the midst of oedipal development.

This monograph explores this state that occurs and the processes that are active in this *moment* of uncertainty in development. When I refer to this *moment*, I am not referring to a moment in time. I am referring here to a *moment* in a process, the process of development. That *moment* in development can persist for a moment in time or for months or even years.

My goal in this monograph is to help the reader to envision and even experience that moment. It is not my intent to discredit or disprove other models and perspectives of development and psychoanalytic work. Other perspectives are important, helpful and even essential in understanding psychoanalytic work and development.

I include in these models and perspectives those of Sigmund Freud conceptualizing psycho-sexual development, Rene Spitz describing organizers (1965), Melanie Klein's conceptualization of the depressive and paranoid positions (1975), Margaret Mahler's enumeration of successive steps of separation/individualization (1975) and John Bowlby's study of attachment (1969). As well, there are empirically derived models from researchers such as Harry Harlow (1970), Arnold Gesell (1925), Gyorgy Gergely (1992) who have painstakingly documented and cataloged the consecutive gains observed in growing infants and children. Although I make reference to some of these schemes and observations, *these details are not the focus of this monograph.*

APOLOGY AND REQUEST FOR LONGANIMITY

I am proposing a different way of thinking about the deep processes of the mind and of development. This new perspective of development that I wish to convey here adds important elements to other models of growth and maturation. Once understood, *this perspective of the moment provides new and powerful ways of grasping and assisting maturation*, one of the central goals of psychoanalysis.

In proposing a new way of thinking, I face the challenge of choosing terminology. If I use new words, I face the daunting task of building an entirely new lexicon which will then be open to interpretation and modification taking years. On the other hand, if I use terms familiar to the readers, these words will carry with them already formed meaning that are useful in trying to describe the new concept; however, these familiar terms also bring all sorts of baggage that I do not mean them to imply.

In addition, finding terms not filled with meaning is difficult if not impossible here since my target audience for this monograph is knowledgeable and experienced individuals who are interested in learning new perspectives and new ways of understanding and approaching the human mind. That audience will likely have read much and have many associations to terms such as development, growth, maturation and uncertainty, terms that I have already used in my discussion here.

Therefore, *one of the greatest difficulties in conveying the concepts of this new model is the language and terminology*. In any case, I have chosen for this monograph a middle path using well-worn words but also introducing new ones. I will do my best to define the terms I introduce and connect them to terms and concepts from the literature where applicable. I will make reference to the definitions and limitations of familiar and well-worn terminology. Of course, when I am finished with this monograph, there will still be work to do to elaborate and further understand the relationship between the new model and concepts, and the known ones in the literature. In other words, I am proposing new territory to add to an old map.

In this monograph, I ask the reader for tolerance and consideration since there will be much uncertainty as I introduce these terms and proceed with this explication of the *moment*. The tolerance and consideration I am asking for is in relation to the many perspectives and understandings that each reader will bring to this discussion. If readers can examine and re-examine their own biases and perspectives particularly in relation to their own affective responses, they will be able to obtain the most from this piece of writing. I provide this apology and ask this self-examination for a very important reason which I will now explain.

One of the underlying tenets here is that *the moment is a necessary part of normal development*. That is to say, we all experience it in the course of growing up and maturing, even into old age. And in fact, each of us experiences this state over and over throughout our lives as we move from one level of development to the next.

Psychoanalytic clinicians are familiar with maturation from a pre-oedipal paradigm to an oedipal one, or from an adolescent paradigm to an autonomous adult one. Re-organization occurs. And we know that in the midst of this re-organization, disorganization, frustration and uncertainty are all part of that process, even when it goes smoothly.

A second tenant here is that *the moment as a state of disorganization with its attendant uncertainties and frustrations is extremely dysphoric.* In fact, I will argue that this state of disorganization can be one of the most dysphoric states that a mind experiences. To give the reader a preview of that which I am discussing, I ask the reader to consider what has been written in the literature about human experiences of nothingness, meaninglessness, chaos (Chessick, 1995; Grotstein, 1990a), and annihilation anxiety (Benveniste, Papouchis, Allen, & Hurvich, 1998a). I would also add external manifestations of these internal states such as confusion, depersonalization, derealization, disorientation, disordered thought, thought disorder and even psychosis. I ask the readers longanimity in considering these internal and external states as continuums of experience and manifestations of the *moment.*

Let me explain. Consider together these two tenets of universality and dysphoria of this process that I am calling the *moment.* Another such state that is uncomfortable and common, although less than half as ubiquitous, is childbirth. *Just as with childbirth, we can not easily call to mind the experience of the moment.* Because of the discomfort, we reflexively distance ourselves. And just as with childbirth, with this *moment* that we have all experienced, *we work considerably hard to distance ourselves from the experience after it is over.*

In addition to distancing ourselves, *the recording of a disorganizing process itself is difficult if not impossible.* For example, think about the state of a technology center recording its own activities. If we implement new technology, recording the process of reorganizing while we are reorganizing is impossible: with what do we record and where do we record it while we are taking down the old recording equipment and putting up the new?

It is therefore an additional tenet of the *moment* that one of the impediments to conveying this new model is this: *even though all of us have experienced the moment repeatedly, we poorly record it even in our memories and what we do remember we reflectively distance ourselves.* This is true as well for the analyst trying to observe the *moment* because the analyst's empathic experience with the reorganizing processes of the analysand will be dysphoric in its recognition in the analysand as well as in the disorganized memory it evokes in the analyst's own development. If there is not conscious awareness of his own experience of dysphoria, the analyst will distance himself from and fail to record his patient's experience.

When the analyst is able to get in touch with the dysphoria and tolerate his own experience of the *moment*, the analyst's empathic experience of the disorganization is itself disorganizing, both in experiencing the analysand's experience and manifestations of disorganization, as well as in the analyst's own past experiences of disorganization that are evoked. Notice I did not refer to the analyst's past experiences as memories. Past experiences of disorganization can be experienced as states of the body, but not as organized memories, as these experiences themselves by their very nature are not organized into memories with meanings. Rather, they are experienced only as states of the body. However, with a clear concept of the *moment*, and a practiced ability to tolerate the disorganization, one can learn to recognize, identify and even hold on to the experience, even as an untranslatable (one that can not be articulated) experience.

These two experiences of dysphoria and disorganization, therefore, create a huge impediment to conveying the concept of the *moment*. Likewise, grasping and using the concept of the *moment* in psychoanalytic work is a challenge for a great many if not all clinicians. (I do not exclude myself in this challenge.) This challenge is not because the concept of the *moment* is so complex or difficult to understand. The concept of the *moment* really is quite simple. It does, however, require one to stand in a different place, listen differently, and tolerate considerable discomfort and disorientation.

At this point, I want to make two disclaimers. The first is that I specify psychoanalytic work in contrast to the more general psychotherapeutic work. I do not mean to exclude psychotherapeutic work in general, but rather wish to point out the deep and lasting nature in working with the *moment*. With an understanding of the deep and lasting nature in working with the *moment*, one may more easily see psychoanalytic process.

The second disclaimer is that although I use extreme cases to demonstrate the concept of the *moment*, I do not mean to imply that all *moments* are extreme. Just as medicine has found and explicated normal functioning through studying pathology, I mean to illustrate the *moment* where the effects are exaggerated. In the final chapter, I will explore and speculate how the *moment* occurs in normal development in which there are incrementally small additions to the model of the world, a bit at a time. These small additions, then, do not create such catastrophic effects. Nonetheless, sensitization to the presence of the *moment*, even when more subtle, can assist in the deep developmental work that deep psychological processes, such as the psychoanalytic process, affords.

PURPOSE

While the nidus of this monograph is psychoanalytic work with psychotic individuals, it is important here to say that my purpose in writing it is not to provide special techniques and parameters that are needed in the analysis of thought disorder and psychosis. In Chapter 3 I do give an example of how one might approach a psychotic analysand, which I hope is useful in illustrating my work. However, my goal in writing this manuscript is to demonstrate where disorganization in its continuum—disordered thought, thought disorder and even psychosis—connects with normative development.

From this perspective, special techniques are not necessary to address such cases as those who are psychotic. Rather, with this manuscript, I hope that the reader will begin to conceptualize thought disorder as a normative process in development and eventually will be able to see thought disorder in all of its gradations from a tantrumming toddler to a psychotic adolescent. Even these manifestations are on a broader continuum that occurs in normal development, that of disorganization at an earlier developmental level in order to re-organize at a more mature developmental level. During that reorganization thought is disordered, even if momentary.

Thought disorder and its extreme form, psychosis, can be conceptualized as a phenomenon of normative development stuck in a meta-stable state of disorganization. With this perspective, working psychoanalytically with a psychotic adolescent is assisting this individual through a developmental transition; something with which all child psychoanalysts are already familiar. From this perspective, analysis of a psychotic individual is not so extreme. Sitting with a psychotic individual although disorienting, bewildering and even frightening, becomes more tolerable for clinicians with this new perspective of the *moment* who can recognize the process as a normative one and help it move along.

In addition, sensitized to the *moment*, subtle movements in development can be more easily observed. Clinicians attuned to the *moment* will see these processes both in clinical cases as well as normal everyday development in children as well as adults. That is, the *moment* does not necessarily, not even usually, present with dramatic disorganization. There are, however, telltale signs that allow one to literally observe development in action. *In understanding the moment, development becomes much more apparent.* With the lens of the *moment*, tracking development becomes much easier, clarifying the psychoanalytic process.

HISTORICAL PERSPECTIVE

Now that I have set the task of this monograph, let me provide a historical perspective. As the basis for this study, I want to consider organizing as one of the mind's primary functions. Bertalanffy (1952), an embryologist, noted that all living things are characterized by two features: organization and primary activity. "This organization is not predictable from, deducible from, or reducible to prior lower-level conditions; for example, a small change, sometimes called the tipping point, lead to a novel, nonlinear shift in organization. In this approach, adaptation is conceived as being complexly governed by the active engagement of a self-organizing biological entity with its specific environment. The emergence of new organizations and forms results from the dynamic processes of assimilation and accommodation engendered by these transactions." (Demos, 2008)

Adaptation is development. The above quote can then be translated that *development is not simply a matter of stimulus and response or cause and effect; it involves the emergence of new, novel organization.* Now, consider the mind in this adaptation/development. The mind organizes information, and perhaps more fundamentally, affects and drives. In development, the mind organizes itself. It is a *self-organizing* entity. *In meeting developmental challenges, the mind reorganizes itself to adapt and accommodate to, and reconcile itself with newfound realities.*

The mind does all of this with the goal of making meaning. With meaning attained, the mind then knows how to proceed, which is likely the evolutionary pressure that pushed it to evolve—with a meaningful way to proceed, the mind maximizes survival of the individual. This is adaptation (Weiss, 1949). The closer that meaning is to reality, the better the chances for surviving and thriving. So there is likely an evolutionary advantage in maximizing the meaning as close to reality as possible, which is why reorganization to match newly acquired information is so important.

In this conceptualization of the mind as an entity that organizes, there is a paradox, however. How is it that an entity that organizes can organize and reorganize itself? That is a central question here and I propose that we consider the *moment* that I have described above.

What I am proposing is not entirely new, as others have pointed to similar processes. Erikson (1956) considered the re-organization that the ego had to do in order to meet the developmental challenges of adolescence. Certainty many observers of children have noted that there is usually a period of regression just prior to a developmental leap (Kris, 1956). For example, a child who has learned a good deal of language, will regress in their language ability around the time of toilet training.

Another relevant thinker from that same period is Bion (1962, 1963, 1965) who talked about beta elements as "undigested facts" and I would include unprocessed affect. In the context of the *moment*, beta elements and processes are a way of describing the dis-organized model and the process of reorganization to a state where things become ordered and connected to one another. In Bion's terminology, alpha elements and alpha processes pertain in this new and improved model of the world that development wroughts. Although Bion does not explicitly introduce affect, he seems to introduce this entire way of thinking in order to circumnavigate strong affect which disrupts the digestion of beta elements into alpha ones.

Wallace (1970), a sociologist, described 'mazeway re-synthesis' both of a social order and of the individuals involved in the process, noting that this re-synthesis is motivated by an outmoded social order and is accompanied by a general disorganization, if not chaos, before a re-organization can occur and allow the society's return to a productive state. Wallace notes that the individuals that lead this re-synthesis are often considered crazy or psychotic until their re-synthesized perspective takes hold. Then this re-synthesis is considered the social order of the day. He notes that this process is reiterative historically.

Attachment is also relevant here (Bowlby, 1969), but not because it was considered integral to Erickson's, Bion's or even Wallace's work. In fact originally, Bowlby's thinking was excluded from psychoanalytic circles. I introduce it here because Bowlby's thoughts were formed at the same time historically as Erikson's, Bion's and Wallace's, and because we now know the importance of attachment in development. I am proposing here that attachment also has particular relevance in understanding the *moment* in development.

Although in different fields, Wallace, Erikson, Bowlby and Bion were writing during the same period and were all thinking about development of the mind. At the same time, there was a great deal of psychotherapeutic work being done with psychotic individuals. Consider the work of Lyman Wynne (Gottschalk et al., 1988) and Harold Searles (1961, 1976) and the work at Chestnut Lodge, Sheppard Pratt and the Yale Psychiatric Institute (Arieti, 1966). All of this work considered the centrality of the mind.

Historically, what came next in the mental health field was the introduction of the Diagnostic and Statistical Manual, Version 3 (DSM-III) (Association & Association, 1980) in which psychoanalysts, psychoanalytic thinking and a belief in the power of psychotherapy were put aside in favor of an empirical behavioral approach, side-stepping the concept of the mind. In the past 30 years, interest in the mind has slowly returned (Levine, 2012). Our knowledge of early child development and the importance of affect and attachment has also increased greatly in the last thirty years. I propose here an integration of this more recently clarified knowledge of development with the previous work mentioned above to provide a new paradigm of development.

In this new framework, just as Wallace and Erikson proposed, *chaos and disorganization are part of the normal developmental process of reorganization leading to maturation.* This new paradigm positions chaotic thought on a continuum that extends to psychosis. By the end of the monograph, I will extend this model of development to include autistic spectrum phenomenon and post-traumatic symptoms in the context of normal processes.

Psychosis, autistic spectrum phenomena and post-traumatic symptoms are of course undesirable outcomes, but my thesis here is that these situations are cases in which the normal processes get stuck in a metastable state and do not proceed. I will present clinical material to examine these situations and offer detailed observations and mechanisms as to how these normal processes get stuck in these metastable states. I will also suggest ways to observe and understand the processes so that they can be used in a clinical setting to move the individual through the necessary reorganization.

THESIS AND SUMMARY

To begin, I propose a thesis which is explicated in the rest of the monograph. I suggest that *there is an identifiable moment that occurs normatively as an individual moves from one level of maturation to the next. This moment is the fulcrum around which development occurs. If one can recognize this moment and the forces around this moment, one can then begin to imagine how to facilitate this moment to gain forward movement in development.*

The *moment* itself is a state of disorganization in the process of happening. The forces around the *moment* that effect the course of the *moment* include (1) unprocessed affect which may be identified by the presence of anxiety, (2) attachment and (3) an organizational process and line of development that is particular to each individual.

Consider a developmental challenge and the *moment* in which an individual confronts this challenge. For example, consider when the oedipal child discovers the fact that he cannot have the opposite sex parent for himself; or the adolescent discovers that he cannot have all the advantages of adulthood without giving up the advantages of childhood; or he discovers the real burden of independence as he leaves home and goes off to college; or the challenges of intimacy as an adolescent loses his first love.

There is much contained in each of these *moments*. *Both from a cognitive as well as an emotional perspective, the challenge contained in each of these moments is to take in new information and create a new world in which this information makes sense.* The individual must make new meaning of this new information. It is like a puzzle that must be assembled in order to reconcile all the information, and all that the individual previously thought he knew with what he suddenly newly discovers to be true. All of this must be done as the individual holds at bay all of the attendant anxieties that come with these new discoveries, and the uncertainties of not knowing what the new world order will look like or bring.

Take the analogy of a jigsaw puzzle. Once the puzzle is put together, a picture is revealed. Imagine that the picture provides meaning and without the constructed picture, there is no meaning, perhaps not even a reason to exist. Without meaning there is no sense in continuing in life since there is no place to go, nothing to do. One's identity, one's understanding and a map of the world, an understanding of what the person wants to do in his life and where he wants to go with his life, in the next year, in the next day, in the next *moment*—in essence, the meaning of his life—is revealed only after the puzzle is ordered. However, the individual must set himself to the task of putting this puzzle together even before he has a reason to move forward. The role of attachment is to hold the individual steady as he accomplishes this task.

In Chapter 2, I take as my starting point for this exploration psychoanalytic work with a psychotic individual, where this reorganizing of the mind can be viewed in an exaggerated form up close and in slow motion. Using a case of a psychotic adolescent, I illustrate a *moment* in development as the mind comes in contact with a piece of reality with which it has to contend but has not heretofore been able to do so. In this *moment*, new material from reality is presented to the organized mind and the mind must reorganize to accommodate it.

In that *moment*, the mind must disorganize to re-organize. Thoughts are disordered in order to re-organize. If the response is overwhelming anxiety because the new information cannot be reconciled with the old model as in the case of psychosis, a kind of malignant chaos ensues as the mind is caught in the midst of re-organizing but is not able to carry through with the reorganization.

Overwhelming anxiety leads the mind to reject that which is being presented to it. Yet the new material cannot be rejected because of the pressure of development. You can never go backward in development (regression is not backward development). Disordered thought then becomes thought disorder.

Through the process of psychoanalysis, the young man I present in Chapter 1 is helped to inch his way out of the disorganization and re-organize his mind to accommodate the new reality. The thought disorder resolves and his mind reaches a new level of maturation. Psychosis, the state of the disorganized mind stuck, is now ended.

In Chapter 2, armed with a sensitivity to this *moment* in development when the mind is faced with integrating a novel facet of the world (including oneself), I examine the analysis of a young child who faces the world with unusual capacities but also unusual sensitivities. These sensitivities expose him to perceived dangers with which his parents are unable to help him. Without their help, he cannot create a model of reality that allows him to navigate in the world safely. In the psychoanalysis that proceeds from this case, we view the developmental process as the child re-organizes his mind so he can access the world in new expanded ways.

In this case also, we can see the disorganized/disordered thought in the process of re-organizing. With the help of the analysis, through the reorganization, the child learns both cognitively and emotionally to process and order the world differently. With this, he is able to move forward in development because now he can take in and metabolize his perceptions to make meaning that is safe and acceptable. With development resumed, he leaves behind his pervasive developmental delay.

In both these cases, there are high levels of anxiety which disrupt the individual's ability to process and reorganize the world. However, there is a difference between the cases where the adolescent has a more persistent psychotic state and the child exhibits self-limited, although quite extended tantrums. The difference is in the developmental stage at which each of these individuals are attempting to traverse.

For the young child, in the context of his dependence on his parents, the parents protect him and do not allow his disordered thought to degenerate into a state of malignant chaos. Whereas, the adolescent's developmental stage is one that necessitates a separation from the parents. Without his parents structure imposed on him, his initial disorganization creates anxiety, further reducing his organizational capacities, leading to yet more chaos with a downward degenerative spiral ending in complete collapse of the ego.

With these two cases, however, I demonstrate the same principle. Reorganizing of the organizational capacities of the mind is a process that can be conceptualized and viewed with each progressive step in maturation. Conceptualizing a progressive re-organizational process in development leads me to propose a super-ordinate developmental line of organization. A super-ordinate developmental line of organization is useful not only in conceptualizing the form and function of the mind for theory building, but also is useful for clinical purposes. *A super-ordinate developmental line of organization assists in tracking the leading edge of maturation*, and it places the development of an atypical child and a psychotic adolescent in a context of a normal developmental sequence.

Stated another way, the psychotic adolescent and the atypical child are stuck in the middle of the process of normal development. They are stuck in the *moment*. The analytic situation helped these two individuals to get unstuck and move through the *moment* to reorganize the mind to the next progressive level of maturation. The stuck state, this meta-stable position is created and sustained by overwhelming levels of anxiety, preventing metabolism of newly found information.

Chapter 3 elaborates on this proposal of the *moment* and a super-ordinate developmental line of organization (A. Freud, 1963) by considering the role of attachment (Bowlby, 1969), affect and its vicissitudes (Fonagy, Gergely, Jurist, & Target, 2002) as essential conditions for the developmental process to proceed from the *moment*. I also consider that the individual facing this *moment* is facing it with an organizational structure that was previously in place.

That organizational structure includes a mind, which has as one of its key components, a body. Here I introduce the concept of the embodied mind (Varela, Thompson, & Rosch, 1991). Fantasies, ideas and models of the world are encoded in the mind with the body being a key component of that encoding process. Affects, drives, and attachments, which may be organized or not, must also be encoded somehow in that organizational structure. *Understanding the body as part of the mind decodes the mind-body paradox and allows an appreciation that disorganized experiences are held in the body which is accessed differently than other parts of the mind.*

In this regard, Freud's note that the body is the first ego (1923) is a useful concept here. So too is the embodiment hypothesis (Varela et al., 1991) in which we can have experiences that are not organized but are encoded as unprocessed data without meaning. These data are Bion's beta elements. These unprocessed elements have been observed and studied in post-traumatic stress phenomena and are an essential component in our understanding of the *moment* (Matthis, 2000).

Heuristically, as a way to orient the reader to a working model of the *moment* and the processes that operate around the *moment*, I introduce General Complex Non-Linear Systems Theory (Galatzer-Levy, 2009). The properties of this model help us to conceptualize, explore and explicate the structure and function of the *moment* as a system of changing states as the individual moves progressively forward in development.

Up to this point, I have written about processes in the mind and body, but make no reference to the brain or neurobiology. In contrast, in Chapter 4, Susan Sherkow offers a refreshing additional perspective. Using principles of neurobiology, she explores both the psychotic young man in chapter 1 and the young child in the second clinical example, providing an additional view of development.

In Chapter 5, I use excerpts from three additional cases to demonstrate how this model of the *moment* applies in two cases of trauma and in a case where there are biological (structural brain) challenges to the organizational capacities of a mind. In the first two cases, a psychologically traumatic event accompanied by overwhelming affect in the adolescent interferes with the reorganizational process in adolescence. One of these cases involved working with an adolescent and the other with an adult with a history of trauma during adolescence. These cases point to the clinical usefulness of the model of the *moment* by illuminating modulation of affect as well as providing organization, and the resultant movement forward in development. In these *moments* demonstrated in the two cases of trauma, the analyst oscillated between providing structure and providing emotional support which helps modulate affect.

In the third case, in contrast to the first two, a pre-adolescent child, devoid of a corpus callosum from birth, initially expresses little affect and is devoid of social capacities, both symptoms most likely influenced greatly by the absent corpus callosum. In this case, the psychoanalytic work involved lending organizational capacity to the adolescent as well as lending fuel (affect) to the developmental process, which then moved development forward.

This material is briefly presented to demonstrate the clinical usefulness of attending to the affect, attachment and organizational processes of development, in short, the *moment* that is worked and reworked in development. The analytic technique and process that is being observed is a refinement of Paul Gray's close process monitoring (1994) and in this way it tracks the leading edge of development.

Finally, in Chapter 6, I summarize the observations and conceptualizations that center around the idea that there is a *moment* that occurs normatively in all of our lives, and is the fulcrum around which development occurs. How we move forward in that *moment* depends on the organizational processes to which we have access, our ability to tolerate and metabolize the raw, unprocessed affect which confronts us, and the support we have (and need), including ego support, as mediated by our attachments. The symptoms of psychosis in an adolescent, developmental delay in an autistic spectrum child, trauma suffered by an early adolescent, and alexithymia in a pre-adolescent who lacked a corpus callosum can all be understood in the context of normative maturation in the context of the *moment*.

My conclusion is that the newly proposed model of development can then be used to find one's way into the *moment*, recognize it, and through an attachment, either lend cognitive organization or affective modulation as the clinical moment in the *moment* dictates. Which action is the correct choice is guided by attending to the states of the mind represented both in mental activity and in bodily expression, and depends on whether the level of affect is creating disorganization that can be tolerated or disorganization that is becoming malignant.

Chapter One

Psychoanalytic Process in a Psychotic Adolescent

The *moment* and the processes occurring around the *moment* described in the introduction can be vividly witnessed in the psychotic adolescent, highlighted against the dramatic changes seen in normative adolescent development. In this chapter, I give an example of psychoanalytic work with a psychotic adolescent to illustrate this point.

As controversial as psychoanalytic work with psychotic individuals is, this is a well-worn and cherished tradition by a number of people (Arieti, 1966; Garrett, 2012; Gottschalk et al., 1988; Knafo, 2012; Kocan, 2012; Koehler, 2011; Lotterman, 2011; Marcus, 2012; Scott Janssen, 2012; Searles, 1976, 1961; Slevin & Marcus, 2011; Stone, 2012). Others have put this work in a broader context of working with meaninglessness (Chessick, 1995; Grotstein, 1990a, 1990b, 1991). My observations of myself and reflections of my own work in this area has given me an appreciation for the anxiety that the analyst faces in doing this work. It is not for the faint at heart. This work, however, becomes much more approachable and tolerable if the processes involved are understood and guided by the developmental context of organizational mastery. The goal of work with psychotic individuals can then be framed as efforts leading the person to move along in normative development, which is one of the foundations of child psychoanalysis (Miller, 2002).

THE CASE OF JAY

Around dinnertime I received a message on my answering machine: Jay, a 19 year old young man had just been brought home from college. I returned the call and heard very anxious parents who were able to tell me little about their son except that he had recently broken up with his girlfriend, had become very upset and was unable to function at school. After speaking with the parents, I spoke briefly with Jay who seemed subdued and responded with one word answers in a voice devoid of affect. I told him, as I had his parents, that I would see them first thing the next day.

The young man robotically hung up the phone, walked up to his room and stabbed himself in the neck. His reason, as he told me months later, was that he had been given the go-ahead in his conversation with me to proceed with what he knew he must do. If he spilled his blood, he would leave this world where men are good, women are evil, and he would enter a new world where he would become a woman, where bad becomes good, and so he would become bad, which was good. Then all would be well, and he would no longer have pain and suffering.

Six months earlier, Jay had left his mother's home and gone off to college as a promising musician, bright and curious. He had been writing music and playing guitar since elementary school. Then, in the midst of leaving his family and trying to establish himself separately at college, as well as trying to work out the intimacy of a heterosexual high school relationship, he lost his bearings, tried valiantly to organize his world according to the letters and numbers from book covers, personal messages from pictures and *Star Trek* episodes which he interpreted as communications from another world.

In doing this, he finally organized his understanding of his world enough to come to the true meaning of his life. That meaning lay in killing himself and being reborn. It had to be this as he could no longer bear the burden of both meaninglessness and unrelenting anxiety, although at the time he was consciously aware of neither of these feelings.

Three years after his initial presentation to me, he is off all medication, has no hallucinations although is quite aware that his thoughts sometimes become disorganized around strong affects, and he is quick to pick up on this and quickly rights himself. He and I now talked about his emerging identity and the developmental challenges of intimacy that are normative for late adolescence. He is productively searching for meaning to his life and finding it in his role as a musician and composer/producer of music; a normative process for young adulthood.

We continue to examine the many ways his early identification with his beloved homosexual father, who raised him, collide with his heterosexual urges. We can also see the ways his exceptional auditory sensitivity and his auditorily organized world (both his internal world and his representations of the external world) contribute to his remarkable musical abilities, as well as the strengths and vulnerabilities of his general organizational processes.

What happened in between his initial presentation and three years later was a five-day-per-week analysis. After stabbing himself in the neck, he was hospitalized and placed on a neuroleptic and lithium. I saw him shortly after discharge and as is commonly the case, he had already stopped his medication, and was refusing to take it. Rather than struggle with him about this, we began the work without medication.

In the first several meetings with Jay and his parents, I gathered as much of the confusing (and I add in retrospect, woefully incomplete as it will always be) history. I also educated them on low expressed emotion (Gottschalk et al., 1988) (which, by the way, is as effective as medication) and helped them to understand the signs of thought disorder so that they could assist in monitoring the progress of our work. Thereafter, for the first 18 months, he was brought five days a week by a family member. He came willingly. In addition, I saw the parents at least weekly, sometimes more to support them and gather feedback as to how he was progressing.

About a month into our work, Jay asked if there might be something he could take that would help with his extreme anxiety and "crazy thoughts." He, then, of his own desire, again began medication. At first we used a very small dose so as to not overwhelm him with side effects. Gradually under my supervision, he increased his dose up to 1 mg Risperdal and 600 mg Lithium daily at its maximum, which is significantly below standard doses for psychosis, but nonetheless was effective in helping him enough so that he could do the psychoanalytic work and tolerate his anxiety. Going above this dose left him with side effects that were intolerable to him. The mainstay of the work, however, was Jay talking about his thoughts and perceptions.

At first his verbal productions were slow, and sparse, interrupted by frequent pauses and staring. Although he denied hallucinations at the time, he later confirmed both visual and auditory ones. He had difficulty articulating words. Sentences were short with simple structure. Thoughts were often incomplete. Much of the time, I could not make sense of what he did say as much as I tried. Disorganization was expressed in his body as well as his mind. In addition to his speech difficulties, bodily movements were awkward, stiff and jerky. His posture was rigid. There was a paucity of movement in general.

He talked about the devil being a woman, and wondered whether or not he was homosexual. Early in the work he noted that if only he were gay, that would make his life easier. He was overwhelmed by his heterosexual urges, and unable to negotiate these feelings with what he identified as his feminine mannerisms and homosexual urges.

He also struggled with whether or not to make contact with his ex-girlfriend. Jay gradually became aware of what his mother told me on their first visit, that he seemed to become disorganized when he had contact with his girlfriend. I later understood the genetic origins of this symptom; as a child, he became disorganized when he had contact with his mother, whom he recalls as chaotic when present but who for much of the time was missing from the family home.

Gradually, in the analysis, his ideas became more coherent. As I sat there day after day feeling lost and confused by what he was saying, I wondered if I was doing anything useful. However, during my three days of absence after four months of treatment, it became clear that his daily talking in my presence was essential for his recovery. During my absence, despite our planning to talk on the phone, he was unable to keep our phone appointments. His voice mailbox became full, indicating to me that he was not keeping up with his normal mailbox hygiene.

In my absence, he again attempted to stab himself in the neck. Fortunately, this time it was only a superficial cut to the skin. He was hospitalized for the last time. On my return, he was discharged. When I asked what happened, he told me that his talking to me every day helped him organize the world so that it made more sense. Without me, he said that he again had lost his way.

At that point in the work, his cognitive processes were still quite disordered and our daily meetings were essential to keep that disorder at bay. As we resumed our work, he continued to reconstitute. In that process, both he and I were becoming more aware of the sensitive topics that would disorganize him. Armed with the experience that exposing this disorganization actually organized him, we pushed on, tolerating disturbing impulses as we became aware of them.

I conceptualized this work in three steps:

1. *Waiting patiently while we gathered data.* This was the most uncomfortable time for both of us. It was clear that at times, especially in the first 18 months he struggled with raw chaos, at times having difficulty with his speech, difficulty forming sentences or keeping his mind on a single thought between the beginning and the end of the sentence. At times I became aware of my own almost overwhelming confusion and anxiety as I sat with him and could not attach any meaning to this anxiety.

For example, he told me apropos of nothing I could connect to it except his own internal impulses, that he wanted to 'fuck his sister.' Another time, he reported he wanted to stab everyone in his family, but could not come up with any reason as to why he would want to do that. Sometime later, he told me that he actually had a knife that he would "dance with," trying to decide what to do with it. Only much later in our work did he have any inclination that he was considering suicide or homicide. But as long as he continued to express these thoughts, we seemed to have some guarantee that he would not act on them, although this understanding is only in retrospect.

2. *We gradually gathered enough information to begin to make meaning of his affects, urges, thoughts and feelings.* The chaos began to yield first to a kind of simple organization of good and evil, then to a more nuanced understanding of himself, his interactions with others, then his understanding of others, then memories of interactions between him and others, particularly his family and later his developing friendships. My presence was important as I lent him my organizational structure which only happened through his attachment to me.

He presented me with disconnected pieces. As he presented these pieces to me, there seemed to be no affective attachment or inherent organization to them. There was no necessarily correct way of putting these pieces together, although there were certainly ways of putting this information together that would not match reality. But it was even in the questions I asked that I was aware of providing him structure, calling his attention to some aspects that were salient to me and others that seemed less important to him. In my lending him my organizational structure, I was aware that someone else might organize his material differently. Nonetheless, if the organizational structure that I lent him matched what he himself could confirm through his bodily experiences, then meaning would begin to coalesce for him and the overwhelming anxiety lessen. He was willing to consider what I offered due to his attachment to me.

For example, sandwiched between telling me how much sleep he had gotten and what he had for breakfast, he told me he wanted to stab everyone in his family but had nothing else to say about it. I wondered with him about feelings that might motivate this thought, and speculated that he might be angry at them for something. That prompted him to talk about a tree in his backyard. He had written songs about this tree which was associated with good memories during his childhood even as it was infested with bugs. His mother had recently cut this tree down and he was feeling as though everything he knew was disappearing including his family, his childhood and now this tree with his memories.

3. Finally, *the meaning of all of this became incorporated into his understanding of the world and eventually it became a part of who he was.*

This process resonated in his hallucinations, his dreams and later in his work, which was creating music and writing songs. For example, in his dreams early in the analysis, he would transform from himself into the devil. Green, which he called evil, would begin to leak onto the walls and threaten to cover everything. Yet there was no meaning to be found, no source of distress, only anxiety. He would become frightened and overwhelmed. Again, *his attachment to me allowed him to tolerate these feelings, especially as he saw that I could tolerate his feelings.*

As the analysis proceeded, *he was able to grab hold of his thoughts and feelings and hold on to them as he could wonder about them, think about them, puzzle through them.* This was seen, for example, in his dreams where he began to be able to remember the elements of his dreams, think about their meaning to him, and put them together into a coherent understanding, which at the beginning had not been possible even with his waking thoughts.

About eight months into the analysis, he began to write lyrics, compose, and play his music, which he had been doing before his psychosis. Later in the analysis, he described the psychoanalytic process as similar to his creative process around music—*he would feel himself untethered as he experienced himself and his world as perceptions that were chaotic, overwhelming, affect ladened but without meaning.*

He felt defenseless as these meaningless perceptions permeated him unimpeded. For example, early in the work, he was anxious in creating his own music, frightened that the music that conveyed his feelings would penetrate others and induce the experience in others that he himself had suffered. As we both survived and later tolerated his states, his psychosis and his anxiety at creating his music also abated.

The chaotic perceptions gradually coalesced into organized constructs such as chords, rhythms and other qualities of the music and he became aware of particular and specific emotional states (sometimes many) that often were distinctly connected to particular experiences in his life, resonating in both the past and the present, like the structure of a dream. Some of his distressing childhood and adolescent memories eventually found themselves expressed in his music.

Much of this music engendered images and feelings that challenged the listener to create meaning, the way that his present would challenged him to create meaning. Some of his pieces presented the hallmarks of psychosis: clanging, loose associations, neologisms, ambivalence and telegraphic, autistic like communication. Beyond that, some of these compositions provided an opportunity for his audience to experience his disorganization and disorientation in trying to make meaning of the world.

These pieces can be thought about in contrast to a coherent model of the world. It is a tribute to Jay that he was able to record and bring to us what I asserted was impossible in Chapter 1, to record the disorganization/reorganization process. For those readers who are interested, a particularly striking audio recording reflecting his conveyed experience of psychosis is available on request (Jay, 2011).

Through the psychoanalytic process, Jay and I came to understand the pieces of the developmental MOMENT for Jay that had to be reorganized. His father, initially one of a couple presenting themselves to the world as heterosexual, raised Jay and his two siblings from infancy. Jay's recollections of his mother are notable for her absence both physically and psychologically reflected in the absence of her from his associations and the paucity of early memories of her.

When Jay, who was the youngest of three, was eight years old, and his older brother was reaching puberty, his father became depressed and withdrawn. Again, Jay's attachment to his parents was challenged. By the time Jay was 13, his father had recovered from his depression and resumed the gay lifestyle that he had had prior to his marriage. Jay's father had also left the family. Without his mother or father. Jay was left to negotiate his own development, guided only by his older brother who had his own struggles, going from a *Dungeons and Dragons* 'Emo' to a crew cut frat boy.

Now, three years after beginning our work, Jay talks about how lost he felt as a child when his father withdrew, how he felt himself to be a grown-up when he hung out with his older brother and brother's friends, but how he so desperately wanted to belong somewhere, and at the same time was overexposed to sexually explicit, violent and frightening material from his older brother and his brother's friends. Finally, even this relationship with the brother he knew disappeared for him as his brother transformed from an adolescent in a world of *Dungeons and Dragons* to a strait-laced crew cut all-American college drinker.

This environment was a set up for Jay who came to his adolescent developmental *moment*: His early identification with his homosexual father collided with the heterosexual urges he experienced in his first sexually intense and intimate relationship with a girl. With insufficient attachment to support him through this developmental *moment*, Jay became stuck in a meta-stable disorganized state. *This developmental moment relentlessly occurred over and over for him, each time he tried to establish normal adolescent relationships the same way Groundhog Day reoccurred over and over for Phil Conners in the 1993 movie of the same name (Ramis, 1993).*

For example, Jay would be with his friends and notice that he had made a gesture, and suddenly he would hear persecutory voices; he would feel confused and experience depersonalization and derealization. As the analysis progressed, when he noticed these gestures, he recognized them as his father's mannerisms, exposing his identification with his father. He identified these mannerisms as feminine, which made him anxious and led him to identify himself as 'probably homosexual,' even as he experienced his heterosexual urges.

Another example was in his intimate relationships. After a year in analysis, he met another girl. He described being quite attracted to her, wanting to touch her, smell her, get physically close to her and have intercourse with her. Soon he began having intercourse with her, frequently. However, when there was difficulty in the relationship, he suddenly began to think about being with a man. Then he would begin to talk about being a homosexual. Later, we came to understand his loneliness when there were difficulties in his heterosexual relationship and his longing for the closeness that he had experienced with his father and longed for with his mother when he was a toddler. This father of the toddler was also associated with his images of god which had been part of his presenting psychosis.

At the core of Jay's normative adolescent development was the challenge for independence from his parents. Normatively, adolescents face this challenge and organize themselves with less parental assistance than in latency, but parents who nonetheless are present. For Jay, however, he had not had sufficient organizing influence from his parents during latency and even less so as he faced adolescence. When he was not able to meet his difficult, overwhelming developmental challenges, disorganization ensued. He was not able to navigate his world, his relationships or even rudimentary planning for himself. Without outside organizational capacities, desperate attempts at resolutions led to bizarre solutions, which are the symptoms we attribute to psychosis.

I understand this to be the reason that psychosis presents in adolescence and not earlier. Adolescence is that stage of development where the child must leave the parents' orbit and without the parents' gravitational forces to help the organizing processes to develop, the adolescent is more vulnerable to the toxic effects of chaos than is a younger child whose parents are never far away.

Adolescence is a time when the intensity of feelings, particularly sexual feelings, increase due to sex hormones and an upsurge of the drives. This increased affect makes adolescents vulnerable to disorganization. Jay's early identification with his homosexual father clashed with his own heterosexual strivings to create unprocessed and unprocessible (for Jay trying to process it alone) affect that was brought to the fore with an intense sexual relationship that in other circumstances would have been normative. It was a normative, expected developmental *moment* for a late adolescent, but because Jay was unable to contain and resolve the normative developmental *moment* and there was no one to assist him, disorganization led to heightened anxiety which led to further disorganization which finally led to complete collapse of the ego.

In thinking about this developmental line of organizational processes as a matter of course in everyone's development, one would expect to see small challenges to one's internal organization which would lead to a small amount of disorganization, next compensation and then development of new capacities of the mind to organize in the face of progressively and increasingly stronger feelings as adolescence progresses. Mayes describes this as an oscillation between chaos and order (2001). Increased conflicts and challenges, and perhaps sensitivities to disorganization, leaves individuals such as Jay at more risk of being overwhelmed by affect and a process that feeds back on itself and leads to complete disorganization and thought disorder when there is a paucity of attachment early in adolescence. As adolescence proceeds and the developmental challenges to separate from one's parents intensify, normative developmental challenges become overwhelming for someone like Jay.

In closing this chapter, I want to emphasize the normative developmental processes that were analyzed. If this case had been presented with an emphasis on his relationships with his mother, father, sister, brother, and girlfriend across development, and these past relationships were put into perspective with his present life experiences and functioning, I think most would agree that this was a deep and productive analysis that dealt with normative developmental tasks.

The fact that the disordered thought processes were brought into bold relief, as I have done in this presentation of Jay, highlights the development of organizational processes. In the analytic work, the fact that the analyst was aware of the disordered thoughts, and tolerated them, even welcomed them, allowed the analyst as well as the analysand to achieve a deeper exploration and analysis of Jay's inner world, and the development of his organizational processes. I have encountered numerous adolescents in the analytic process in which the disordered thought and even psychotic processes are not apparent to others, but nonetheless are present in their internal world. In Chapter 6, I offer two examples.

Chapter Two

Psychoanalytic Process in a Young Child with a Pervasive Developmental Disturbance

To restate my thesis for this monograph, the *moment* occurs normatively in all of our lives as an integral part of the maturation from one developmental stage to the next. The *moment* is present when thoughts are not ordered and affect is unprocessed, and is the fulcrum around which development occurs mediated by attachment and an organizational line of development particular to each individual.

Chapter 1 describes the *moment* and the processes occurring around the *moment* in a psychotic adolescent. The analytic work with Jay demonstrates the developmental nature of the disorganization in the face of an unresolved developmental challenge, that of establishing sexual and personal identity. Through the attachment with the analyst, the analyst's tolerance of anxiety and the analyst's organizational support, Jay reorganizes his ego and then resumes normal development.

The case of Jay demonstrates not only a psychoanalytic process that leads an analysand through and out of psychosis, but also the normative nature of the "moment," even if stalled by an unresolved developmental challenge in which the analysand dispenses with reality to find a temporary solution. The reader at this point will likely say, "Of course disorganization and reorganization in a psychotic adolescent is expected. And even if the *moment* can be demonstrated in a psychotic adolescent, this does not demonstrate the ubiquitous nature of the *moment* in development." In this chapter, I use a case of a four-year-old child to illustrate the *moment* in the development of a young child.

THE CASE OF EVAN

Evan presented at 3 year 10 months as verbally precocious. For example, when helping him to get dressed, his mother would carefully lay out 2 sets of clothes, both reasonable for the weather and his age. When given this choice, he would say to his mother that this was not really a choice since it did not include the clothes that he wanted to wear.

Evan was also struggling with a *moment* in his development that had been going on for some time. As an infant, Evan could not tolerate more than one other person in the room at the same time (here is the *moment*) and would react even more intensely if another child was in the room. He was noted to have this response from the time he could crawl. He would move off to the edge of the room and hide his head, facing the wall or commence a several hour long tantrum or begin tearing the room apart when he was older. After his sister was born when he was about 2 years old, these problems worsened and his parents became anxious that he might attack his baby sister.

This crescendo in intensity led his mother to seek help for herself. The referral for Evan then came through the mother's therapist who informed me that Evan was having frequent and intense tantrums. This therapist also felt it important for me to know that Evan's mother had grown up in a physically abusive household. This issue had come up in mother's therapy as she struggled with what to do with her aggressive toddler, and was reluctant to be forceful with him.

As my work with this toddler and parents began, Evan retreated to the bathroom whenever I came to the waiting room to invite him in to my office. It took several months of sitting with Evan as he huddled against the wall in the bathroom outside my office before he gradually became comfortable with my presence.

After a while, Evan, his mother and I all moved in to my office. As I sat on the floor in my office, eventually Evan approached me. Soon thereafter, he began leaning on my thigh as I sat cross-legged. Once installed in my office and comfortable with my presence, he was able to use me in an attachment. Initially he brought me his beloved choo choo that had been a gift from his father, his father's childhood toy that Evan cherished but was unable to keep safe from his own aggressive outbursts. Evan asked me to hold his choo choo and keep it safe. Here was the first developmental task that he brought to me, which was to help him bring his aggression under his own control.

I came to understand this process that moved him from the bathroom floor to the intimacy of my office and his asking me for help as reflecting his presenting difficulty in attachment. With my help, he now had an attachment that could supplement the one he had with his parents. Even still, if I was away for two or three days, it would take him a few days to again become comfortable with me.

As I puzzled with what made it so difficult for Evan to be comfortable in the presence of another, Evan began to take an interest in folding paper airplanes. In our folding the planes together, I quickly discovered that although he so urgently wanted to learn how to make the planes, he could not tolerate me helping him. If I even touched his paper, he would trash it and begin again. He struggled mightily to follow my every move and in a few sessions was precisely copying my actions with considerable dexterity. He took great delight in folding more and more complex planes.

Initially in flying the paper airplanes, he was anxious as to where they would go. But as we learned to control their flight to some degree and take joy in their unpredictable nature, he seemed to be more comfortable with his own trajectory in space. For example, in one session his father was sitting in the room focused on some computer work. Evan folded a plane and designed it in such a way that he threw it in one direction and by design it veered off and hit his father, consistent with his strong conscious wish to get his father's attention. In less than a month, we had learned to fold at least 15 different models, and in six months he had completed at least 50 different models, each with its own characteristic flight idiosyncrasies, including a couple he had designed himself.

There was something remarkable about the way this child understood and organized space. I came to appreciate that this spatial sensitivity and his ability to organize space was amazingly developed but also left him vulnerable, as he reckoned space between him and others so precisely and was constantly feeling violated by those who did not share his precision. This had left him crippled in the use of his attachments that might otherwise support his development.

In the meantime, his aggressive outbursts continued and soon were brought in to the office. Sometimes these tantrums were triggered by having to keep him from hitting his younger sister as she entered my office, wanting to play with my toys. Sometimes they were triggered by his mother asking him to get out of the car to come to my office, especially if I had been away for a few days prior.

Once a tantrum started and if he was unrestrained, he would run around my office grabbing and throwing anything he could reach. If there was any attempt made to restrain him, his screaming would increase in intensity and he would throw himself about. The tantrums would continue for the entire session and in these *moment*s, I found it difficult to think. Although usually his mother and sometimes father was in the room, I found myself restraining Evan. As I did so, I noticed that once I had him safely and securely held facing away from me, he would relax and the room became more organized.

If I let him go, however, he would likely resume his wild, out-of-control, disorganized behavior.

Initially mother was at a loss as to how to approach him. Although she was cognizant of how well she had been able to protect and care for him, she was frightened to use her physical body and her own physical power to guide him and organize him when he became out of control. Here is the *moment* in the child's life that resonated with a *moment* in his mother's life. Evan's chaos resonated in his mother through her remembered experiences of the physically abusive household from her own childhood. Perhaps this is also a glimpse at the intergenerational transmission of the psychological mechanisms that manage (in this case ineffectively) disorganization/anxiety/aggression/abuse/violence.

Neither Evan nor his parents had been able to organize his unprocessed affect which resonated with his mother's unprocessed affect. The *moment* would spiral out of control, function would break down and solutions could not be found, despite both mother and child being highly intelligent. As in the case of Jay's parents, Evan's mother was not able to be present to bring her organizing parental influence to bear in order to organize herself as well as Evan. Nonetheless, his parents had been able to structure his life and contain his affect enough so that other significant portions of his development continued even prior to my contact with them.

As I observed mother and child, I noticed that when the *moment* would occur for Evan (and these occurrences were frequent) his organizational processes would degrade. When his mother attempted to come in close proximity to him to help contain the overwhelming unprocessed affect (as would be the usual adaptive response in a normally attached mother/child dyad at this age), it had the opposite effect in Evan of creating even more anxiety. His mother then responded with increased anxiety. Neither Evan nor his mother were able to contain the anxiety and Evan would erupt into behavioral chaos.

As I approached Evan to assist mother and restrain him in the middle of a destructive tantrum, I discovered that if I held him facing outward, he did not become more wild. He calmed. I attributed this to his not being overwhelmed by his spatial sensitivities. With instruction and coaching, mother gradually learned to hold him firmly in the same way. In this manner, we developed ways of organizing Evan's world to compensate for his spatial sensitivity. The safe restraint structured him enough and allowed him to use his attachment to his mother and me to organize himself.

This restraint allowed him to organize but was still somewhat noxious and in a relatively short time, under tremendous pressure from within, Evan developed his own strategy: he would be about to have a tantrum and suddenly would have a determined look on his face, say resolutely that he would manage this one himself, and run to a safe place in the room where he could talk to himself and settle his anxiety. After this, he could resume.

Notice that he incorporated past successful techniques. A social component of talking to himself and communicating to others had been added to his previous strategy of going to the edge of the room. His successful use of this organizational strategy early in life was modified and adapted to a more mature level of self-control of his aggression. This more mature level now included not just a defensive and self-protective component but also a social component—one in relation to his attachment figures.

As this process of self-control was added to his repertoire and soon thereafter became internalized, he began to interact with other children. After a time, he developed a friendship and routinely began to play with the girl next door. Soon they were engaged in cooperative play. Then suddenly, in a *moment*, one day, completely out of the blue, he hit her. This happened several times.

Then the same *moment* resonated in his relationship with me. He and I were playing an older version of peekaboo in which he was hiding under my coffee table and poking his head out of one side and then the other. In response, I got on top of the table and met his gaze first on one side, then on the other.

He found great delight in being able to see me when I was not anticipating where he was. We danced back and forth in this way for a time. Then we began to modify our timing, which became even greater fun. In these modifications, however, suddenly he found my face a mere six inches from his. An instant later he swung his fist at me as hard as he could.

Although he clearly became anxious after he hit me, with the work we had already done as a foundation, he and I were able to bring the chaos under control quickly, do a post play analysis and move on. Soon he learned to do this on his own. Here again, the spatial sensitivity had overwhelmed him, but now with the organizational capacities he had learned and his use of me as a secure attachment, we were able to put the problem into words and solve it.

After 13 months in analysis, he entered a pre-K program, did well with 25 other children in the room and has continued to flourish. In the context of the analytic work, Evan, his family and I found various solutions that allowed him to not only weather the *moment*, but evolve to the next level of organization. So here we see an example of a *moment* in a toddler who has special sensitivities. These sensitivities made him vulnerable to the challenges of development in a number of ways including the difficulty in making use of his attachments in the developmental process.

The same situation likely applies to other children who are challenged developmentally in their ability to attach, such as with children in the autistic spectrum. In this way, we can see that attachment is important in helping the child tolerate and contain the anxiety of the *moment* we are describing, and in helping the child formulate solutions and construct a new system, evolving to the next level of development.

The manifestations of this unresolved *moment* for Evan were uncontrollable tantrums rather than psychosis as in the case of Jay. Let us consider where Jay was developmentally compared with Evan. A normative adolescent is challenged with independence from the parents, and must organize himself with less parental assistance than a toddler who must by necessity have his environment much more structured.

When Jay was not able to meet his developmental challenges, disorganization ensued. He was not able to navigate his world, relationships or even rudimentary planning for himself. Without outside organizational capacities, desperate attempts at resolutions led to bizarre solutions, which are the symptoms we attribute to psychosis.

I understand this to be the reason that psychosis presents in adolescence and not earlier. Adolescence is that stage of development where the child must leave the parents' orbit and without the parents' gravitational forces to help the organizing processes to develop, the adolescent is more vulnerable to the toxic effects of chaos than is a younger child whose parents are never far away.

Chapter Three

A Model of the *Moment*

The Introduction provided an outline of this monograph and introduced the idea of the *moment* as a developmental challenge in which the organizing mind reorganizes itself to accommodate to newly found information. Chapters 1 and 2 provided clinical examples of the *moment* in the cases of a psychotic adolescent and an atypical young child with spatial sensitivities. This chapter steps back from the clinical situation to ponder a conceptualization of the *moment*.

In order to explore the *moment* conceptually, I first consider the four key elements that have been introduced in the Introduction and through the clinical material thus far:

The *mind organizes* all that it knows into a model of the world so as to make meaning. With the meaning, the individual can navigate through the world in a purposeful way.

The process of maturation involves taking in new information that does not fit the old model of the world. This new information throws the old model into question leaving the individual without purpose or direction. This leaves the organizing capacities of the mind disorganized. In order for maturation to proceed, these *organizing capacities must be reorganized.*

Affect is both the motivator for the maturation process and also an element that itself must be metabolized in the maturation process. Too much affect in its pre-cognitive, unmetabolized form can also disrupt the maturation process.

Attachment is a necessary element that helps modulate affect and provides external structure and organization, facilitating the maturation process.

Next, I bring these four key elements together and introduce the model of *a super-ordinate developmental line of organization.* Then, in order to provide a way of thinking about this model as a dynamic process, I introduce *General Complex Non-Linear Systems Theory* as an overall conceptual frame for development. Finally, in this chapter, I return to the clinical material and consider how this conceptual framework can both contribute to our understanding of the clinical material and inform us of how to proceed in the clinical work.

THE MIND AS AN ORGANIZING AGENT

Let's begin with a conceptual question, "If we consider the *moment* when a person confronts new information about themselves and/or the world and is on the verge of creating a new model that incorporates this novel information, what happens?"

As the person confronts new information, his state is one of disorganization. From a cognitive perspective, the developmental challenge is to take this new information in this disorganized state and create a new model in which the novel information is organized in relation to the old, making meaning of the new information. It is like a puzzle that must be assembled in order to reconcile the new information with all that the individual thought he knew before the new discovery.

For illustrative purpose, we may take an extreme example using the analogy of a jigsaw puzzle as one's model of the world. Once the puzzle is put together, a picture of the world is revealed and meaning can be made. But in this *moment* of disorganization, the puzzle is in pieces. Without the constructed picture, there is no map to the world or to life. There is no meaning, no reason to exist. Without meaning there is no sense in continuing in life since there is no place to go, nothing to do. One's identity, one's understanding and a map of the world, an understanding of what the person wants to do in life and where to go with life, in the next year, in the next day, in the next *moment*—in essence, the meaning of life—is revealed only after the puzzle is ordered.

Now ponder the *moment* when a developmental challenge occurs and the puzzle that the person thought he had assembled is suddenly discovered to be in disarray when a piece is discovered that makes the previous sense of the puzzle meaningless, or at least throws the sense of the known puzzle into question. The person is left without meaning until the puzzle is reassembled with the new piece incorporated. Anxiety is created when the person becomes aware that he must re-assemble this puzzle before he can orient himself to his new world in which he comes to terms with his new situation, finds meaning in this new existence and can proceed.

Without assembling this puzzle, there is no direction, no source of motivation. In this *moment* the person is on the edge of chaos. In this *moment* on the edge of chaos, the constructed picture of life, one that has given meaning to the life, suddenly comes into question. In the initial instant of the *moment*, there is disorganization, a sense of something not known and an imperative to make sense of it. This disorganized state creates anxiety, in some cases so extreme as to be called annihilation anxiety (Benveniste, Papouchis, Allen, & Hurvich, 1998b).

What a person does with this *moment* in time to address the *moment* in the process determines what happens next. If, in the face of this anxiety, the person patiently sits down and begins to work on the puzzle, the individual gradually reassembles a more useful model which resolves the developmental challenge posed by the new information. With this challenge resolved, meaning can be made of the newly discovered information and the individual can proceed in life.

However, if the individual is overwhelmed by anxiety, he may back away from the challenge if he can. If forced by internal or external circumstances, his capacity to put this puzzle together degrades. In either case, the individual is not able to proceed in life because the working model of the world is now in at least two pieces that have no relation to each other.

If this state of disorganization and its resultant anxiety continues, cognitive capacities are further compromised creating even more anxiety. This positive feedback loop engenders more and more anxiety which engenders more and more cognitive disruption. This positive feedback loop is just as a fire feeds on itself; the hotter it gets, the more it burns and the hotter it gets. If unchecked, this downward spiral leads to complete collapse of the organizational capacities. In other words, the ego breaks down.

The scenario that I have just described is an example of an extreme situation in which the new information is felt to be tied to essential components of one's world model. What I have tried to portray is a schematic that shows the connections between development, organization, disorganization, and meaning. In most cases, this maturing process is an evolution and not a revolution. That is, rather than a cataclysm, there is a dialectic between order and chaos (Mayes, 2001). The changes are taken bit by bit, dissembling small pieces of the world model at any one time. Nonetheless, these transformations must take place in maturation and development. And sometimes these changes are cataclysmic as has been illustrated in the above examples.

But even in the less cataclysmic case, there is an important dimension that has not been acknowledged by the pedagogy of psychoanalysis, although I believe is reflexively done by good clinicians. The missing dimension is that there is a real limit to the human mind in the process of development, a limit in the mind's ability to organize. If pushed beyond that limit, the organizing capacities of the mind begin to break down and nothing beyond that limit is productive.

In working with children, I frequently hear from parents, teachers and judges that the child "has to learn" this or that. When pushed beyond the mind's limit, defensive processes are usually if not always engaged. The defenses protect the individual from breakdown, but frequently anger those around him. The real situation in many of these cases is that the child is expected to function beyond his organizational capacities. The child cannot and will not learn, not because the child is being willful, but because the child has not developed the organizing capacities or the ability to tolerate the level of anxiety necessary to address this developmental challenge.

I extend this observation to adults as well. Sometimes an adult is seen as "being defensive." The defensiveness, however, may be protecting the individual from breaking down. It is in analyzing these defenses that analysis proceeds, not in discovering what is on the other side of the defenses (P. Gray, 1987). One way of understanding the analysis of defenses as Gray describes it is that it allows the analysand time to accommodate to and then metabolize the affect. Once that is done, then there can be a cognitive engagement that organizes new found pieces of reality. In other words, analysis is helping the analysand develop organizational capacities and metabolize previously unmetabolized affect in the face of previously unintegrated information.

As clinicians, it is critical for us to search for that organizational limit even as the limit may change *moment* to *moment*. It is knowing this limit that will allow the clinician to help guide her charge to an optimal place in the process of development. In finding that optimal place, the key is attending to affect, just as Paul Gray describes (1994).

AFFECT

Just as the mind is the organizer as well as the organized, *affect is the fuel that drives development as well as the substrate upon which development operates*. When I use the word 'affect,' I mean something more than emotion, more along the lines of what Matthis has described (2000). Emotion has meaning. For example, we use the words *sad* or *happy* and they have meanings. However, imagine a person who has been overwhelmed in reaction to a perceived event. The overwhelming affect that is experienced is unprocessed and is stored in the mind as primary sense perceptions, visual, auditory, tactile, proprioceptive, olfactory and even gustatory. This affect, however has no meaning, no place in the mind where it fits into a narrative. Without meaning, the individual has no sense as to how to respond to these stored but unprocessed sense perceptions.

Affects can be stored in memory as raw sense perceptions in the body, devoid of meaning, awaiting processing. The study of trauma has demonstrated that these sense perceptions can be stored in a raw form devoid of meaning (Kaplan, 2002). Post-traumatic flashbacks are the mind re-presenting these perceptions to itself in an effort to try to metabolize them. These properties of affect apply to development as well as trauma. Processing or metabolizing the affects consist of taking these sense perceptions, organizing them, giving them meaning and arranging them into a narrative. These raw sense perceptions are like 5 second clips of video material, each meaningless on their own but gaining meaning when assembled sequentially into a movie (Matthis, 2000).

Freud's comment as the body being the first ego is apropos here (1923). The concept has been extended by Johnson (1987) and Varela et al (1991) who suggest that the mind is not just housed in the brain, but also in the body. For example, emotions are experienced and recognized as bodily sensations. For those emotions that are unprocessed, there are sense perceptions of the body that are stored in memory and can be recalled, but have not yet been assigned any meaning or understanding. These memories are uncomfortable because they are experienced but have no meaning. These unprocessed sense perceptions of the body stored in memory generate anxiety because, like an alarm, they put the mind on alert, and yet with this alarm going off, the source of the danger is not specified. The alert can only register potential danger, but does not specify where or in what form the danger comes nor how it can be warded off. Attempts may be made to avoid the memories and yet with danger lurking about, there is an urgency to give these unprocessed sense perceptions meaning. Here, Gray's approach asks the question, "What is the danger?" (1994), seeking to metabolize the unprocessed affect and connect it to meaning.

Varela (1991, pp. 147–184) goes even further regarding unprocessed material saying that not just sense perceptions and affect but even cognition is based on the body itself rather than just a set of logic circuits in the brain. For example, a visual understanding of the world arises from sensorimotor activities and interactions with the world. Through these sensorimotor activities and interactions with the world, we lay down a pre-cognitive visual model of the world based on how we have moved in the world, how we have touched, manipulated and interacted with the world (Johnson, 1987).

In Bion's terms, we are talking about beta, pre-processed elements (1962, 1963, 1965). Bion's terminology is particularly useful here in distinguishing between alpha and beta elements on the one hand, and alpha and beta processes on the other. Affect is both an element and a process in Bion's terms. But we have to make some distinctions that also differentiate our discussion here from Bion's. When Bion refers to elements, I believe he is referring to both information and affects. Both information and affects are necessary parts that comprise Bion's elements. When he refers to processes, he is referring to both cognition and affect. Again both cognition and affect are necessary parts of Bion's processes.

Affect as a Bionian element is metabolized in the course of development. However, the same affect moves the metabolism forward as a Bionian process. If the affect as an element is too great, it overwhelms the process. If affect as a process is too great, it overwhelms cognition and disorganizes the organizational capacities. The more mature the individual, the more affect can be tolerated both as an element as well as a process. On the other hand, if there is too little affect, although the element of affect is easily metabolized, there is not enough affective fuel to motivate or move development forward.

Parens (2011) comments about development are relevant here: he writes about an 'optimal level of frustration' to optimize development, by which I translate to mean 'optimal quantity of affect'. In growth and development of the child, Parens instructs parents (and would-be-parents) on how to use the attachment the child has to the parent in order to modulate the child's affect and provide the right amount of structure.

In the area of psychosis, there has been much work done on environments of high and low expressed emotion (Gottschalk et al., 1988) Again, I would translate emotion to the word I am using here, *affect*. Environments with high expressed affect have a disorganizing effect on psychotic individuals. I would add that environments with high expressed affect, if high enough, will disorganize anyone as in situations of psychological trauma and even in the case of Evan as his tantrums disorganized me. Also, consider that young children are more vulnerable, by which I mean, they are more easily disorganized by intensely experienced affects.

Unprocessed affect that is stored as a memory in the body is a key concept in this monograph, and also in psychoanalytic thinking. To begin with, it answers Freud's question about the existence of unconscious guilt. This unconscious guilt is held as unprocessed affect. It also speaks to Spitz's Coenasthetic experience of the infant (1945; 1965), but extends that to not just the infant experience, but to all human experience. The coenasthetic experience is unprocessed material held as sense perceptions in the body. Bollas also has written about this unprocessed material as the "unthought known" in which he describes "how experiences affect the child without the child being able to process this experience through mental representations" (1987).

The concept of unprocessed affect is a key concept in the "*moment*" for important clinical reasons as well because *if affect is stored and manifest in the body, then reading the body becomes a critical and indispensable part of working with and analyzing the moment.*

To restate what has been covered thus far in this chapter, *the moment is a state of mind in which unprocessed affects held as sense perceptions, beta elements in Bion's terms, exist but without meaning*; the stored sense perceptions, the raw experience is not yet metabolized into a known experience. There is an urgency, even a desperateness to make the experience known and thereby make it meaningful. The basis of newly forming cognition may also be locked in this pre-cognitive state when newly encountered experiences that do not fit into the known world model held by the individual are encountered. These primary sense perceptions, however, can be unlocked in the context of an attachment.

ATTACHMENT

The term 'attachment' usually brings to mind Bowlby's work with mothers and infants (1969). When I use the word here, however, I mean something more. I mean to expand Bowlby's definition and make it more general. This new definition includes a process that occurs throughout development, not just between mother and infant. *By attachment, I mean to refer to a process involving another who provides affective modulation as well as lends structure and organization to the individual experiencing the "moment."*

I am including the concept of auxiliary ego, but not just for survival and not just to be used, but used specifically for the purpose of development in the moment. I also mean to include what Sugarman referred to as a developmental object (2003). This concept brings in the role of the parent for the developing child. The term 'developmental object' has been considered in contrast to the analyst's function as providing interpretations. My use of the term 'attachment' invokes both functions of developmental object and interpreter which are necessary both in development as well as in the psychoanalytic situation.

When I am referring here to the psychoanalytic situation, I am not just referring to child analysis. Although many analysts, especially those who are only trained in adult work may not want to admit that they provide this developmental function. Loewald freely writes about this developmental function in the termination process (1988). In contrast to Loewald, Gray's approach of close process monitoring (1994) emphasized the analyzing part, which in my terms would be providing structure and organization. However, there would be no traction in the analytic process if attachment did not occur.

By the use of the term 'attachment', I also mean to emphasize a human connection that must be felt by the analysand and allowed, if not supported, by the analyst. I additionally mean to specify the functions of affect modulation and lending organizational support as key activities for the analyst in this role. In many cases, these activities are done by the analyst as a reflex to seeing a person begin to disorganize and spiral toward chaos. My goal in writing about this process is to make explicit what many analysts are already doing.

In the case of clinical work with trauma, where the subject is not able to organize sense perceptions (Lewis, 2012), the therapist functions in two ways (Bacciagaluppi, 2011). The first is providing a place that is experienced as safe. In providing a safe place, affect is being modulated, in this case reduced. Furthermore, the therapist structures the process by slowly uncovering the unprocessed data, collecting this data and helping to structure this data into a coherent narrative, all organizing and structuring functions. However, these techniques are effective only if the traumatized subject accepts these functions which the analyst performs. The acceptance by the analysand is what I am pointing to when I use the word *attachment*.

We can see another aspect of attachment when we compare the case of Jay, a psychotic adolescent with the case of Evan, an atypical child. Because of the dependent nature of the young child and the attachment that connects the child and the parents, even when the child who is overwhelmed by his own high-intensity affects falls into a chaotic state, as in the case of a tantrum, the parents re-orient the child to reality. The child accepts the parents attachment since the child is dependent and has no other means of survival.

On the other hand, the developmental challenges of the adolescent's push from the inside and pull from the outside create a demand that the adolescent organizes himself. Without the parent present, if the organizational capacities are overwhelmed by intolerable affect, there is nothing to prevent a downward spiral in which the disorganization reduces the adolescent's capacity to tolerate and process the affect. Without a reliable and effective attachment, high intensity affect is more potent in disorganizing. This comparison of the presence of the attachment in a toddler versus an adolescent is a compelling argument as to why schizophrenia presents in adolescence rather than earlier or later in development.

If we consider the psychoanalytic process as a process of development (Greenacre, 1975), we can see the critical importance of attachment both in development and in the analytic process. In these two cases of Jay and Evan, we see how attachment modulates affect and makes it tolerable for the developing individual. In fact, the analyst is critical for survival of the mind. I am also speaking of the sense of survival of the body. Recall the embodiment hypothesis discussed above in which the body is a part of the mind. The disorganized body in a very real way is the disorganized mind which senses that it is breaking apart. This has been talked about in the literature as annihilation anxiety (Hurvich, 1989). In many cases, attachment to the analyst allows the analysand to tolerate this anxiety.

A SUPER-ORDINATE DEVELOPMENTAL LINE OF ORGANIZATIONAL PROCESSES

Now that four elements key to an understanding of the *moment* have been discussed, let us consider how these elements relate to each other in the *moment*, when the task of the mind in development and maturation is to reorganize itself.

To begin, consider again the analogy of a puzzle and imagine strategies employed in putting it together. For a jigsaw puzzle, these strategies might involve such techniques as grouping together and assembling all of the edge pieces, or finding pieces of the same color or pattern. Of course, these strategies depend on capacities of perception such as the ability to differentiate colors and shapes of the pieces.

Now, imagine a color-blind child unable to differentiate red from green. This child would look for alternative strategies, and would be vulnerable to those puzzles that would require red/green discrimination to assemble. In the same way, in developmental reorganization, the child's constitution matters.

For example, Evan's constitutional sensitivity to space created a vulnerability to being overwhelmed affectively by the mere presence of another child in the room whom he felt to be intruding on his personal space. This vulnerability interfered with his development in many ways including his inability to use his mother as a source of organization when his organizational capacities broke down, as during a tantrum.

The child's development also matters. You would not give a young child a 1,000 piece puzzle to assemble. Rather, you would begin with a simple one or two piece puzzle, and then introduce successively more complex puzzles, fostering the child's ability to develop this organizational process. *The organizational process is then a product of development as well as the child's innate abilities: a developmental line of organizational processes.*

For example, a child who has seen successively more complex puzzles will have much better puzzle assembling capacities than a child who at some advanced age is give a complex puzzle when not experienced with simpler puzzles. Over time and throughout development, the organizational process that I am describing becomes embedded in the child's functioning. Each puzzle that is solved becomes part of that development, and *the organizational process becomes structuralized within the personality.*

In the case of Evan, in his early life with his family, he could not learn to organize his world spatially since these processes were vulnerable to breakdown. However, when the analyst allowed Evan to regulate the space, and then progressively introduced more intense challenges, Evan was able to gradually develop ways of organizing the world so that it was understandable and not chaotically intrusive. We get a glimpse into the workings of that process when, in the game of peek-a-boo, Evan's system was suddenly overwhelmed, his organizational capacities temporarily broke down, and he hit the analyst.

The organizational process also contains within it some capacity to face uncertainty, to decide what to do when a problem that has never faced before is now confronted. This capacity is hard to pinpoint, but we can find an example in the insect world. There is a male moth that finds its female mate by following the gradient of the female's pheromone concentration. The male flies back and forth looking for a stronger and stronger scent of pheromone. The female hides in the underbrush. The male eventually flies past the female and loses her scent. The male does this over and over until finally he does something that he has never done in his life. At the place of strongest pheromone concentration, he drops to the ground and continues on foot through the underbrush until he finds the potential mate. Those capacities in us, when frustrated or challenged, to come up with the unexpected, the innovative, are important.

Finally, we are social creatures. Children are embedded in and require the matrix of parents, family and community for their development. The organizational process includes the child's ability to call in and use this matrix. The child is not just a passive recipient of this attachment. *The child is active and is an actor in the attachment process.* Here the concept of attachment, which was discussed above, is crucial. The role of attachment functions in two ways. When the attachment is working well, as in Parens' parenting model (2011), it modulates affect, especially anxiety. It can both quell the affect/anxiety as well as increase it. In other words, *the attachment at its best can create an affective holding environment* (Winnicott, 1960).

The *second role of attachment is to provide outside structure and organizational capacity when the child's capacities fail.* For example, when a child becomes so frustrated at trying to find an answer but cannot, the child often exhibits anxiety and will frequently ask for the answer. An attachment figure sensitive to the child will step in and provide structure and organization. In the way I have defined attachment here, its overall function is to orient the developing person. *Attachment acts as a beacon, a north star by which to navigate through reality, especially when lost in the storm of chaos.*

GENERAL COMPLEX NON-LINEAR SYSTEMS THEORY AS A MODEL FOR DEVELOPMENT

At this point, we have all the pieces to assemble and get a static picture of the *moment*, but before going back to consider the clinical situation, we need a conceptual framework for how all of the pieces work together; we need a model for the dynamic processes of the *moment*. We can find such a model in general complex non-linear systems theory, also referred to as chaos theory

(Dodds, 2011; Gleick, 1987) and self-organizing systems (Piers, Muller, & Brent, 2007). I will refer to it here simply as non-linear systems theory.

The modern version of non-linear systems theory has its origin in work by Poincaré (1890) who studied the properties of three bodies orbiting each other and found that this dynamic system was highly sensitive to initial conditions. In modeling a three body problem, he found that with minor alternations in conditions specified at the outset, future trajectories varied significantly.

Gleick (1987) alluded to non-linear systems theory, which he called chaos theory, as a paradigm shift (Kuhn, 1962) from the previous stochastic linear paradigm. In the twentieth century and up to now, modern science has been based on the stochastic linear model. The linear model moved our understanding of our universe forward by informing us of properties of populations. Sampling, repeating measurements and using statistics filtered out "random noise" and determined significant elements of "importance." In this stochastic model, the idea that a butterfly flapping its wings on the other side of the earth having influence on major weather patterns was absurd.

In contrast, non-linear systems theory is based on chains of events. In these chains of events, miniscule differences in initial conditions can have cascading effects, potentially changing future trajectories significantly, even catastrophically. In the past 25 years with the advent of high-speed computing, modeling and solving non-linear equations became possible, ushering in an interest in examining non-linear dynamic systems. Although non-linear systems theory is a field of mathematics, it has broad applicability in several disciplines including physics, engineering, economics and biology. For example, in the last two years, weather prediction has become strikingly accurate (Samenow, 2012). In biology in the mid-twentieth century, two embryologists Weiss (1949) and Bertalanffy (1952), noted that small random variations early in development sometimes created strikingly different outcomes.

A number of writers have considered the relevance of non-linear systems theory to psychoanalysis (Galatzer-Levy, 2009; Hamburg, 1987; Moran, 1991; Spruiell, 1993). The usefulness of this theory to psychoanalysis is that there are specific properties of non-linear systems that provide both a metaphor and a model of the mind (Quinodoz, 1997; F. Verhulst, 1999; Ferdinand Verhulst, 1994). One of these properties is evolution (Ghent, 2002; Palombo, 1999) which, in psychoanalytic terms, is translated as development (Levin, 2000; Mayes, 2001; Novak, 2004; Tyson, 2005). In this process of evolution/development, a system approaches "the edge of chaos" (Dodds, 2011), and self organizes (Piers et al., 2007) and evolves, revealing emergent properties. Stern (1983) referred to chaos and unformulated experience, himself referring to even earlier writings (Schachtel, 1959). In these writings, unformulated (unprocessed) experience can also be understood as "emergence" (Galatzer-Levy, 2002; Kieffer, 2007).

The *moment* that I have been describing is such a *moment* when a system is on the edge of chaos. The translation is as follows: The system is the human mind. Evolution is development of the mind, from infancy to old age. The edge of chaos is the "*moment*" of meeting a developmental challenge. *In the context of the moment on the edge of chaos, there is an opportunity for the system to evolve to a higher level of complexity but also the risk of collapse.* This *moment* can be an instant in time but it will extend either until the challenge has been met, or the challenge is backed away from, or the system collapses. Embedded in this *moment* is the unprocessed affect which we can refer to in our General Systems Theory model as excitement or energy. The emergent properties include processed affect and the superordinate line of development which is structuralized in the personality.

Let me give you a visual model which will illustrate. Imagine the inner contour of a bowl as a system, a child at a particular level of development. A marble rolling around inside the bowl locates the child's affective state at any particular instant, and the contour of the bowl is the bounds for all of the possible stable affective states of this child. Imagine that the bottom of the bowl represents the state of the child that is unchallenged, unexcited, unenergized, unfrustrated. As we spin the bowl so the marble rolls, with more and more vigor, the marble moves off the bottom of the bowl and begins to move along the side of the bowl. Yet more vigorous spinning of the bowl brings the marble further up the sides of the bowl. Points further up the side of the bowl are those states in which the child is more challenged, more frustrated, more excited, more energized; in short, higher affect.

When the marble gets up to the lip of the bowl, on the edge of what the child can contain in terms of frustration, excitement, energy, affect, and challenge, the child is "on the edge of chaos." The child's worldview, organizational capacities, ego structure, all described by the contours of the bowl, are at the limit of being able to contain the highly energized affective state of the child. If the marble moves one millimeter further, the child's state will be outside of her known system. The child enters chaos. The state of chaos is the disorganization in the *moment* that I have been describing. Context and meaning are lost.

Chaos is one of the most anxiety provoking and dysphoric states for the mind—and for good reason. In this state, the organism is unable to protect itself as it has no functioning model to detect danger, no model to guide it to safety. The child has gone beyond his known universe because of some newfound information. He must construct a new model which takes time and patience. But since the child is outside of his known system, the sense perceptions cannot be easily organized into an experience, and meanings cannot be attached to the experience. When chaos is experienced, it cannot be immediately resolved. Furthermore, the anxiety generated by the chaos increases the level of excitement. What this means is that the affect, the anxiety, the excitement, the frustration cannot be processed in the *moment*. The *moment* has as one of its attributes unprocessed affect.

From here, either the child constructs a new system represented by a larger bowl to contain the higher level of excitement, energy, frustration, challenge, anxiety, affect, etc., or the child is lost to disorganization. In the terminology of non-linear systems theory, either the old system is constructed into a new system with a higher order of complexity and ability to contain more energy or the old system collapses. In Jay's case, when he began a downward spiral of anxiety and cognitive disorganization, I would lend him my structure, allowing him to contain the higher level of energy and avoid collapse so that he could construct his own new system and structure.

How does that construction of the new system occur? Here what we have said about how the developmental line of organizational processes applies. There are constitutional capacities, a line of development of organizational processes, the ability to do the unexpected and attachment as a guiding hand that participates in that construction.

IMPLICATIONS FOR THE CLINICAL SITUATION

What I have described here in the development of organizational processes can also be viewed as processing the affect and making meaning. Now consider again the three steps in the process of analyzing Jay through his psychosis:

1. Waiting patiently while we gathered data. This was the most uncomfortable part of the process: existing in the midst of chaos, without meaning. This was not just the edge of chaos but chaos itself. A calm abiding presence through an attachment with me as Jay's analyst was instrumental in order to help him tolerate the overwhelming annihilation anxiety. When affective levels were too high, I calmly listened, knowing we had the time of our session to allow the anxiety to settle, and also knowing that if I was concerned about safety, I could rely on the family. It was important for me to not feel anxious since my calm abiding presence was conveyed through posture, tone of voice, relaxed facial muscles, etc.
2. Once enough of the pieces had been gathered, both Jay and I began to make meaning of his affects, urges, thoughts and feelings. When anxiety levels began to rise above a certain level, I would begin to see disorganization, and later he was able to describe anxiety. His degree of organization/disorganization was conveyed in the fluidity of his speech, the sense of his words, even his posture and bodily movements. When I saw the disorganization, I provided an organizing com-

ment, even if it was to say that it was confusing. Sometimes simply a nod would allow him to reorganize.

3. When meaning began to coalesce, Jay's organizational capacities became stronger and he could tolerate more uncertainty.

My work with psychotic adolescents such as Jay and disorganized younger children such as Evan has provided me with opportunities to clearly see the *moment* and with patience, track the development of these newly forming organizational processes. This tracking was done using an understanding that unprocessed affect is stored in the body and its effects can be seen in the body as well. In particular, when the affective load was too great, cognitive processes became disorganized. With Jay and Evan, this could be seen in the fluidity of their speech, thought production, motor planning, interaction with the world and even bodily movements.

As I did this tracking, I was able to see when Jay and Evan were not available to hear an interpretation, were in the state of gathering data but not sufficiently oriented to the data to make meaning, were overwhelmed by the affect, etc. Similarly, many times I was able to anticipate for example, when they were available to tolerate the next step. These are all procedures to which well-trained psychoanalysts can attend.

After navigating the unprocessed affect, the next step is the development of new organizational processes and meaning-making that is a product of the new organizational processes. When I was able to see where Jay and Evan were in the *moment* and whether they could move forward productively, or would get caught in the positive feedback loop that led to chaos and collapse, I could see when I needed to lend my own meaning-making and organizational capacities, or when they were being productive on their own. In either case, my listening presence, the attachment that they used, was a holding environment that modulated the affect/anxiety.

Let me say a little more about this process of lending my own meaning-making and organizational capacity, as I think that many analysts (particularly ones who have not worked with children) would question this. Consider Winnicott's concept of children seeing themselves reflected in their mothers' eyes (Winnicott, 1960, 1971). When it is most growth promoting, the image that the mother reflects is a combination of a realistic assessment of the child's capacities and the mother's own organizing and meaning-making capacities.

Of course, as analysts, we want to allow as much autonomy as possible to the analysand and do not want to impose our own biases. But the child, and also by analogy our analysands, cannot move forward in development without the mother's and our (as analysts) organizing and meaning making capacities as explicated by what I have described occurring in the "*moment*." In addition, consider Valera et al.'s (1991) analysis from a cognitive science perspective, in which the body is an integral part of the mind. From this perspective, the developing mind and the environment, including the mother/other, are not independent of one another.

This interaction between mother and child in the *moment* provides a glimpse into the inner workings of attachment. It begins to answer the questions: What is attachment? What is happening in the attachment process? And why is attachment so important for development? As can be seen in the explication of the *moment, attachment, at least in part, has to do with the need for the mother to lend organizational capacities* to the child, organizational capacities that are so necessary for development. *Attachment is also necessary to modulate the anxiety that accompanies disorganization.* If we believe that psychoanalysis provides an opportunity for development, then we have outlined here the critical importance of this process between analyst and analysand.

In considering attachment, it is easy to see that the organizational support needed at different levels of development will be considerably different. For example, normatively the parent of a young child provides a much higher and more intense level of organizational support than does the parent of an adolescent. And when the young child is confronted with development on the edge of chaos, that more intensive support will prevent the child from going into the downward spiral that leads to complete collapse. Not so with an adolescent. In this way we can imagine that the manifestations of success and failure are different at different developmental stages due to the differing developmental capacities and the differing levels of support available to the child.

In summary, I have considered the *moment* when an individual is confronted with a developmental challenge. That challenge comes in the form of information that disrupts the child's present state of understanding and meaning. This *moment* in developmental terms has unprocessed affect imbedded in it. In general complex non-linear systems theory, the *moment* begins on the edge of chaos, threatening to disrupt the system. In psychotic individuals, the system has been disrupted and has entered a downward spiral in which the chaos positively feeds back on itself and leads to further chaos and complete breakdown. With the help and support of an attachment, however, the developing system, the person, evolves to a higher level of organization, toward maturation.

Now to the relevance of being able to understand and detect the *moment* in the clinical practice of psychoanalysis. The extreme state of psychosis provides a vivid demonstration of the *moment*, but as I have become more aware and more sensitized to the *moment*, it has become apparent to me that this construct has broad applicability. For example, monitoring of the *moment* is what I believe Paul Gray was pointing to when he talked about close process monitoring (1994). I will demonstrate this broader applicability in Chapter 5.

Chapter Four

Neurodevelopment and Psychoanalysis: Discussion of Evan and Jay

Susan P. Sherkow, MD

Psychoanalysts who work with children, especially very young children, approach a patients' diagnosis, psychodynamics, and treatment plan by relying upon their thorough study and understanding of development. Conceptually, the term "development" refers to an array of intertwining trajectories of the growth of an infant that comes from multiple perspectives from conception through old age.

For our purposes, "development" refers to the acquisition of cognitive, physical, and motoric capacities, and learning, social, and interpersonal competencies. "Development" includes the evolution of drive and drive derivatives—oral, anal, genital, gender, and oedipal phases—from the perspectives of both pleasure and aggression. "Development" also describes the process by which the organization of conflict, in the context of a child's object relations and environmental and interpersonal influences, results in his acquisition of defenses and character formation in the form of ego and superego. Lastly, "development" can refer to the neurobiological maturation over time of brain circuits and connectivity.

While "psychoanalysis" is commonly understood to be a process directed at "understanding" a person's inner world, we increasingly are learning about the relationship between observable behaviors and brain function. At the very least, we know that any change in psychological function implicitly references *a simultaneous change in the neurobiological patterns inside the brain.* In other words, our work in psychoanalysis not only addresses apparent feelings and conflicts manifestly expressed in behavior, but simultaneously affects neurological pathways, through plasticity of white and grey matter. It behooves us to think of analysis as a tool to reconnect or rewire parts of the brain that are affected by, and that in turn affect, our actions, feelings, thoughts, and intentions.

To approach understanding Dr. Fallon's work with his two patients, first Evan, and later Jay, we are going to address very specific aspects of functional neurodevelopment insofar as they can help us explain these patients' psychology, symptoms, and treatment. To set the stage for understanding Evan, a toddler who had demonstrated developmental unevenness from his first months of life, we will focus first on the pre-cognition elements of neurodevelopment, then on cognition itself, and then on internalization of experiences.

Firstly, the study of "neurodevelopment" addresses itself to the function of biological substrates of normal and abnormal expressions of emotions, cognition, sociability, and intentionality. The simplest substrate to describe is the component of feelings: the instinctive, intuitive ingredients of relating and being attached. Innate, preverbal, positive or negative emotions become increasingly connected to an object, in all the complexity that emotional connections entail, including sensory responses, emotion-laden memories, stimuli triggers, and what we hypothesize comprise the emotional attachment to mental representations of the object. While infants in the state of pre-cognition are understood to have "implicit knowledge" by virtue of instinct and intuition, the neurobiological development of emotions in an infant is, by definition, yet independent of the connections to the cognitive part of the brain, connections that will enable "explicit knowledge," once myelinization begins to connect emotional and cognitive centers of the brain.

Secondly, cognition (or "thinking") is a formal, innate, gradually emerging process driven by physiology: the laying down of white matter between areas of brain that gives the growing child the ability to use language to represent experience and feelings, and allows experiences and memories of experiences to be formed, stored, retrieved, and verbalized. The evolving language and symbolic systems are in constant flux, as more and more information pours into the sections of the brain which process information from both inside and outside.

The third component of neurodevelopment can be described as the gradual internalization of interpersonal experiences that underlie capacity for social ability. Functionally, through cognition and the growing connections between the parts of the brain responsible for "feelings" and for "thinking," a child appears to process multiple simultaneous messages and actions, as well as stimuli that come from both inside of himself and from the external environment, all of which are constantly being modulated and integrated (Baron-Cohen, Leslie, & Frith, 1985; Fonagy et al., 2002). In shorthand, we use the word "experience" to mean mental, physical, interpersonal, and intentional events of all kinds, understood to be registered as mental representations *neurobiologically* in the brain (Baron-Cohen et al., 1985; Fonagy et al., 2002). The ability to form mental representations, leading to mentalizing one's own thoughts and experiences as well as those of others, functionally referred to as "theory of mind" is essential (Baron-Cohen et al., 1985; Fonagy et al., 2002; Leslie & Thaiss, 1992). An important sub-component of this process is developing the capacity for "empathy," itself dependent on the ability to develop a "theory of mind."

Importantly, then, from the perspective of an analyst studying the brain differences that are invoked in the development of symptoms and anxiety in a child, we would think in terms of the formation of his particular mental representations in a child, how a child registers brain-wise, representations of positive, negative, and conflictual experiences and feelings, ones that promote healthy ego mechanisms or ones that may or may not be "safe" or "manageable."

Moreover, as these representations of experiences come together to create "organized development," they include fundamental organized *expectancies* of what will happen in relationships, in contexts or patterns that are *predictable and dependable.* From birth, possibly even *in utero*, a child begins the lifelong process of organizing and making sense of his experience without words, through interaction and playful communications with his mother, well before he begins learning words to describe his experience.

For every child, an important part of the creation of "organized development" is contingent on a child's endowment: his capacity to perceive, encode, and introject mental representations of his mother according to his own neurobiological makeup and sensitivity, with varying degrees of receptivity and plasticity, under the influence of age-related unconscious drive derivatives. Every baby encodes his experiences of the forces of sucking, biting, genital exploration, bodily exploration, toilet training, and triangulation; these forces are not static, but are subject to change over time, through which emotions, beginning with love and hate, are normatively expressed.

To manage these mixed developmental and drive challenges, and the conflicts they create, a child relies on the intertwining processes of encoding, symbolizing and using language, but these are also dependent on "nurture," internalizing through first introjecting and later identifying with his parents. He then uses these processes to *regulate himself*, by monitoring and then by modulating internal and external stimuli, particularly experiences with his parent. In sum, a typically-developing child relies on his identifications with his parents, and the mutual empathy and ability to mentalize each other, in order to self-regulate.

Even a child on the autistic spectrum (ASD), and certainly a child predisposed to psychosis, proceeds through essentially the same developmental tasks, regardless of how visible or invisible the process may be. When the tasks of development are altered by the presence of a neurobiological difference, such as ASD or uneven development, we see "symptoms" or behavioral differences that obscure the achievement of other normative and equally necessary developmental tasks. We customarily label these behavioral differences as "developmental deviation," or "developmental unevenness," in cases where some tasks are achieved and others are poorly developed or absent, but where a full-blown picture of autism spectrum disorder has not emerged.

Developmental unevenness always results in secondary effects, not only on a child's sense of "self" and sense of "other" but also because significant unevenness can severely impact a parent's sense of safety and security. For example, a toddler might be able to show positive emotion by allowing himself to snuggle, and to initiate a hug, but he might not be able to speak, or might be clumsy. Another child might show a brilliant understanding of classical music and distinguish Beethoven from Mozart, but might frustrate his parent by not responding to his name when being called.

THE APPLICATION OF A PSYCHOANALYTIC/ NEUROBIOLOGICAL PERSPECTIVE TO THE TREATMENT OF EVAN

A psychoanalyst assessing a toddler relies on applying his knowledge of normative developmental schemata and landmarks in order to decode his patients' behavior. He also relies on his intuition to discover that his patient has a "mind" and that his behavior has meaning, no matter how well disguised. Giving particular attention to the details of the world inhabited by his patient, his patient's parents, his home environment, his extended family, and his social and educational network, the analyst takes into account the child's endowment, his physical and psychical competencies, and his temperament; he assesses how the developing psychology of the child has been formed by, and in turn has influenced his parents. In particular, he looks at the role that a mother's emotions, fantasies, and actions have played in the toddler's processing of reciprocal social and emotional interaction, and the mechanisms which have played a part in the toddler organizing and regulating his feelings and experiences.

The analyst will also try to decipher how the toddler represents his good and bad feelings to himself: his overall self-representation as well as part-representations, as lovable, good-enough or not, as capable of certain functions and which ones. The analyst will also use his observations of his patient's behaviors in the office to help understand a child's mental representations of his parents.

Evan, the 3 year old described by Dr. Fallon, presented with an inborn neurobiological difference that is on the spectrum of developmental unevenness, showing a hypersensitivity to proximity. While such hypersensitivities to sensory stimulation can be a component of autism spectrum disorder, they may not be accompanied by the other neurobiological markers of ASD, but nonetheless they produce a syndrome between mother and baby that can be akin to ASD in causing serious disruption of the mother/baby relationship. A baby who is hyper-alert to sounds (like horns or dishwashers), visual stimuli (like lights, eye contact, patterns), tactile stimuli (itchy and restrictive clothing, gritty sensation on the tongue) or, as in Evan's case, proximity may experience the world as adverse.

Hypersensitivity to sensory stimuli reflects an abnormality in brain wiring, and is disruptive to the development of organizing neurological structures; impairment in any area of brain development thus can impact all domains. Moreover, a child struggling with a severe sensory overload will have difficulty processing and thus controlling not only the overload of stimuli, but also processing and organizing his negative emotions. Given that babies try to avoid what they can't process, they behave as if they are instinctively averse to the stimuli, and depending on the form of the stimulation, averse to mother as well. An infant avoids by screaming, having a tantrum, or turning away. While visual overstimulation can be avoided simply by gaze aversion, sensitivity to proximity to mother is impossible to avoid, because a baby cannot be fed, soothed, or changed without it.

In this framework, we know that Evan presented to treatment with a history of uneven development and with this hypersensitivity to proximity. How do we imagine that his hypersensitivity impacted Evan, and how did it further impact his relationship with his mother? In other words, from the perspective of his particular neurofunctioning as a hypersensitive child, how might Evan have experienced and introjected his mother's caretaking in the process of organizing his developmental experiences? And, in turn, how might his particular hypersensitivity have impacted Evan's mother's perception of her baby?

Firstly, not only did Evan appear to have an inborn hypersensitivity to proximity, but his mother was also sensitive to the dangers of proximity as a consequence of her own history of physical abuse. It is not hard to imagine, then, how frightened she might have been to find her child overly sensitive, even averse, to her approach. She would likely read this as rejection, and as confirmation of her worst fears about herself. Evan might then have felt that his mother was pulling away from him despite his need for attachment, because of her misreading of his sensitivity.

Secondly, what strategy did Evan use to cope with the increasing demand for organization of his body-driven experiences? Brains are programmed to organize, and a typically-developing child will develop normative obsessive-compulsive defenses. A child with inborn differences in neurofunction will nonetheless still be forced to organize—but will find seemingly random behaviors to organize his thoughts and emotions, which are just as symbolic to him and just as useful to defend against the developmental forces at hand. Evan appeared to cope by using a mixture of physical avoidance, hiding his face, and by not allowing other children in the room at the same time. When he was overwhelmed, or his boundaries were violated, he would hide his head.

While Evan's aversion to being close was apparently multi-determined, a combination of his innate neurobiological sensitivity and a consequence of the reciprocal maternal/child avoidance, Evan also developed conflict-based symptoms. The least intrusive and destructive of Evan's behaviors was his use of defensive avoidances of various kinds, such as hiding his face, and turning to the wall, to avoid experiencing overwhelming negative feelings that he couldn't process. In this, his behavior seemed to mirror his mother's struggle with her own helplessness in soothing and regulating her child. It may have been that his developmental delay in differentiating sensations compounded by his early use of avoidance also prevented him from organizing his feelings toward two *different* people at the same time. It also seemed likely that the birth of his sibling played a role in his developmental struggles.

Evan may have had further impetus for his ambivalence about allowing his mother to restrain him, beyond his ability to articulate his need for her for containment, by virtue of his being attuned to her reaction to *him*, and thus become developmentally stuck. Mother's sense of helplessness at being unable to help him along with her early experience-driven anxiety regarding aggression imposed uncomfortable affective states on her ordinary mothering experience. Both Evan and his mother's affective reactions combined to create anxiety that overwhelmed both of their abilities to find a solution which in turn created *more* anxiety.

THE THERAPEUTIC INTERVENTION

Evan began treatment by displaying his aversion to proximity and intrusion on his space, huddling in his analyst's bathroom. Over time, Evan began to allow the analyst to move closer, and furthermore he developed the ability to form symbols to represent his terrifying feelings. In Dr. Fallon's office, in the process of developing a therapeutic relationship, Evan was able to give his precious choo-choo to Dr. Fallon to hold, a symbolic representation of Evan's wish to be held and protected. Evan let something precious be held in the office as an expression of his wish and hope to be able to be held without fear of retaliation. This enactment points to Evan's dawning cognitive awareness of his own self-destructive tendencies, an aspect of observing ego that is essential to therapy, even therapy with a toddler. Handing the toy off to Dr.

Fallon was a message from Evan that he wished his mother could be comfortable enough to hold and protect him, and not feel as though *he* was hurting *her* when he became so angry or jealous.

Evan then, in the course of his therapy, developed another way to relate to Dr. Fallon, through the use of modalities that were comfortable and acceptable to him, that is, not overloaded with the overstimulation imbedded in the realm of being close and being held: namely, the normative ability to use his visual field, and his more-than-ordinary ability with proprioception and spatial relations. Applying his precocious capabilities both in folding paper and in organizing space allowed Evan to make a positive connection by making and flying airplanes. However, it took time for Evan to feel non-threatened by the possibility of being "held." While folding paper airplanes, Evan would trash any airplane that Dr. Fallon had contact with. And, later, when Dr. Fallon's face came close to Evan's during their game of peek-a-boo under the coffee table, Evan lashed out in a burst of reactive rage, swinging at Dr. Fallon as hard as he could!

Through the play with airplanes, Evan also could represent his body and possibly his genitals (at this point in treatment, he was in the genital phase), i.e., symbolize moving his body and erecting his phallus in space. When he could make the airplanes "fly away" from him, the play also allowed Evan to master separation anxiety. The use of the observing ego in this implicit separation shows that Evan, too, could observe himself, and it opened up room for play dialogue.

Historically, Evan's development of modulation of affect and of speech had become impaired, and processing internal and external cues had cycled downward in a negative, disruptive, disintegrating sequence, instead of moving toward the "normal homeostatic state" of inner achievement. Through play, Dr. Fallon brought Evan back into the world where actions implicitly have meaning, which allowed a play space to develop between toddler and analyst. In this way, the analyst thus plays a role in enabling a toddler to resume acquiring those major biological schema that have seemed to falter in the parent-child relationship. Importantly, the analytic work promotes the formation of mental representations of each other's play, while together analyst and toddler make sense of the external world by monitoring and modulating the child's internal and external perceptions, and his reactions to them. As Evan's sessions demonstrate, the analytic process applies to any action at all that takes place in the office, including stimulations by sounds and light. It also applies to interactions of any kind with a caregiver that are observed in the office or waiting room.

Such play works to create mutuality and reciprocity, an empathic framework for managing aggressive impulses. Dr. Fallon and Evan were able to work through approaches to negative feelings, allowing Evan to internalize parts of the relationship with his analyst, within the acknowledged boundaries of work in the office. One does *not* want to come close to replacing the parent: a very important part of analytic work with very young children is maintaining a boundary, and helping parents recover their ability to parent.

Technically, an analyst plays with a child in two overlapping play spaces-reciprocal play and watched play. In reciprocal play, a child engages with the analyst just as toddlers play house: for example, with parent and child taking turns feeding each other or taking care of a baby, or putting puzzle pieces together. In watched play, the child directs mother (or the analyst) to stay put and be quiet while he plays, allowing him to project his emotions, especially hostile aggressive emotions, into the play. Such play promotes the child's development of affect regulation by allowing him to construct, reinforce, and internalize mental representations of the analyst's ego-building latent interactive presence (Sherkow, 2004)

We see this in Evan handing Dr. Fallon the choo choo: he relies on the fact that Dr. Fallon has the ego capacity to reinforce Evan's wish to control himself. Dr. Fallon was able to help Evan develop the ability to regulate his emotions through the shared experience of pretend play, which scaffolds his imagination and language and leads to advanced symbolic functioning. In this process, the analyst allows unacceptable impulses and ideas to be projected onto him, or onto objects in the office, with the intention of translating them back to the child (and at times the child-with-parent), so that interactions become meaningful. Being fully attentive, with sustained and focused attention, is an important element in successful treatment, because these children specifically lack the capacity to focus and *stay* focused. Any emotional challenge, whether positive or negative, will prompt them to default into symptomatic behavior, creating play disruptions. Interpretations of these play disruptions on the spot can help re-engage the child to return to the level of symbolic function of "pretending" in play.

In summary, we have an example in Evan of developmental unevenness and the use of an analysis to "catch up." For Evan, allowing another to be close was the most delayed and aberrant area of development, with the ability to manage separation anxiety markedly delayed as a result of this sensitivity. In the course of treatment, as Evan resumed a normative developmental trajectory, Evan's visual-spatial and proprioceptive capacities could be invoked to enhance his ability to engage and express himself as he developed language. Evan's phallic interest then became apparent, even though it was not overtly addressed; it appeared as though, as typically happens, developmental organization, in this case Evan's phallic interest, proceeded unnoticed and unrecognized (possibly even by his analyst), regardless of the other delays. By the time Evan entered school, he had evened out, with all developmental arenas on par for his age.

COMPARING EVAN WITH ANNA

By both comparison and contrast, I will use the treatment of Anna to illustrate the resumption of a developmental trajectory in another child who presented with developmental unevenness, albeit one whose parent had very different sensitivities and vulnerabilities. Anna was sent to me at age 2 ¾ for gaze aversion, limited speech, and frequent rage reactions during which she was inconsolable. She also had a sleep disturbance and food aversions, which her mother took in stride. Indeed, Anna's mother was one of the calmest, most thoughtful and empathic parents I have ever encountered, and comfortable with disciplining her daughter, neither afraid nor judgmental of her.

Anna was a beautiful little girl who used my toys to organize her affects similar to children on the spectrum: instead of using my toy kitchen for pretend play, she spent significant periods of time in lining up plates, cups, and foodstuffs, making sure each lineup was perfect. She avoided doll play, fearful of feeding, undressing them, or making them wet; she was unable to look me in the eye, was upset by any sound, and while she regularly hummed to herself, she seemed terrified if I tried to sing along with her. She was also terrified of noises that, we discovered, included monsters that would attack her at night; scared of boys in her classroom; afraid of her teacher; and backed away from any child she encountered on the playground.

Anna responded extremely quickly to intensive therapy multiple times a week, with her mother present in the sessions. It soon became transparent that Anna was struggling with angry, jealous feelings toward both of her parents, largely derivatives of primal scene and oedipal issues that had been projected onto monsters in the nighttime. Her uneven development seemed to be explained by her extreme auditory hypersensitivity, which seemed to have interfered with processing her negative emotions, which must have seemed particularly dangerous to her, and interfered with her making cognitive use of her precocious but inhibited language skills. Within a month, Anna appeared like a "typically-developing" little girl in my office, although it took another 11 months of therapy for her to catch up on her social skills.

Just when we were contemplating termination, Anna's mother became pregnant, and she panicked about the potential impact on Anna, seeing her pregnancy as a loss to Anna. Mother's own issues of sibling rivalry now emerged, very apparently disorganizing her. Mother's former admirable parenting skills seemed to evaporate, much like someone on the brink of "chaos." Mother manifestly lost her ability to empathize, and amazingly, couldn't "think" how to help Anna cope with a new baby.

Of necessity, we continued the analysis, enabling Mother to cognitively reorganize and enabling Anna to be prepared to accept the new baby. In fact, Anna seemed to adapt more gracefully than her mother, who stumbled on *thinking*, as if she had lost her cognitive capability with regard to processing the advent of a second child. In parallel, she was unable to help Anna *thinking* about the experiences ahead of her, nor to anticipate the baby positively—being a big sister, helping dress and feed the baby, or being mother's little helper.

In due course, I was able to help Mother address her intense anxiety, her identification with Anna as a child about to be deprived, replaced, or discarded. She began to practice thinking about helping herself grow into a new role, a mother who would have to tolerate being shared by two children. This in itself shed light on Anna's struggle with the triad at home; perhaps her mother's unconscious fear of "sharing' had contributed to Anna feeling like a monster about demanding not to be left out.

The shift in Mother allowed her to help Anna grow into her new role as well, reinforcing the work in the analysis. Anna, perceiving a change in her mother, began to enact in her play her former fear (of losing her mother) condensed with her current fear (of being made to disappear by the new baby). While Anna was using a bang-a-ball hammer to push balls into their slots, making them disappear, she stared at me and announced that she had a recurrent dream about wanting to flush her mother down the drain! Her play became increasingly multi-determined in reflecting anal, phallic, and pregnancy themes, consolidating her ability to express herself and manage transitions. Toward the end of Mother's seventh month of pregnancy, Mother and I agreed that Anna could tolerate the upcoming hiatus in treatment and multiple "new" experiences, not only the birth of her sibling but also moving to a larger apartment.

After her baby sister was born, Anna was brought back to therapy for a period of time to prepare for our termination. During these sessions, Anna wanted her mother to sit with the baby in the waiting room, which separated my playroom from my adult office, i.e. one had to walk past them to get from one room to the other. In a remarkable session, Anna began the hour, as she had been doing of late, by preparing breakfast for us, bringing the plates of toy food from my playroom into my adult office, picnic-style. This time, she slammed the door on her mother and sister, leaving them trapped in the waiting room, as Anna put her plates of food on the floor in front of me.

I chose not to call attention at that moment to this condensation of all of Anna's former and current Oedipal and sibling angst, in part because we were about to stop our work for the summer but also possibly longer, and *that* needed to be addressed. Thus, I told Anna that we were going to be stopping for the summer in three weeks, and I showed her the dates in my appointment book. She took in this announcement and continued to make her trips back and forth between rooms, bringing in more picnic. After her third trip to the playroom and back to my office, as she was again heading for the door, I said, "Oh dear, what is going to happen during Anna's vacation? I won't have anyone to bring me breakfast!" She paused for a second, then motioned and said, "Come with me." I understood immediately that this was her response to our impending separation.

Some minutes later, now playing at eating our breakfasts on my office floor, with Anna moving furniture around so we could sit next to each other, Anna said, "Now it is time to go to sleep!" This was play that she typically introduced near the end of our session, and I thought that she must be referring to the upcoming separation. Immediately, she became bossier than usual, giving me many more commands than usual: she lay on my analytic couch, asked for the head towel and the blanket, saying, "Take off my shoes, cover my feet . . . turn out the lights, close the blinds . . . you lay down there—pointing to my sofa—go to sleep!"

Obediently, as I lay down on the sofa, while Anna pretended to fall asleep on my analytic couch, Anna whispered, staring at the ceiling, *"I don't know how to be angry."* "I'll help you," I responded. At that, she jumped off the couch and began collecting our picnic plates, while I made a list for her, *"How to be angry."* As I read the list, Anna instructed me to act out each of the options I had named, such as "yelling" or "crying" or "complaining," giggling the whole while. When I came to reading the option "throwing," I acted it out by throwing a toy cup of toy fruit across the room.

Somehow, when we went to clean up the fruit, we seemed to have lost the toy apple. We hunted for it, completely puzzled; it had to be nearby. As I searched behind the furniture, Anna instructed me to, "Go behind the chair, and hide from the monster! Play monster!" I thus pretended that I was scared of her, the monster, who was going to punish me for throwing and thus losing the apple out of my anger. After several repetitions of this play enactment, Anna then reversed the play, and played that *she* was the one about to be punished by *me*.

In this play, Anna demonstrated her achievement of the capacity to anticipate transitions *and her reactions to them*, thereby being able to organize the impending multiple changes into patterns of the "expectable" and the "predictable." A new psychodynamic/neurofunctional organization allowed for the enactment of monstrous feelings that could be controlled through language and symbolic play. Anna's ultimate request for a means to express and manage her negative feelings reflected the new organization of neurobiological cognitive processes.

In working with children with ASD and developmental unevenness, we have discovered that the *inability to manage transitions* and the *inability to anticipate* play very important roles in their development, stemming from their neurobiological differences. The ability to anticipate a transition from one place or person to the next, the ability to plan, inherent in the ability to think into the future and prepare for the consequences of a change, is diminished. It makes sense that if one can't process one's experience, one cannot achieve the norm of *dependable expected patterns*.

Managing transitions has a trajectory of its own in typical development; transitions may be met with variable anxiety depending upon stage and circumstance. The capacity for "anticipation" itself is a developmental marker that can be observed very early in the first year, when a baby quiets as soon as he sees his mother enter the room, knowing he will shortly be fed. Later, we could imagine that the moment of being on the brink of discovery, or making a connection that had not previously been made, could be "a light-bulb" *moment*, filled with pleasurable anticipation and reward.

The feeling of "anxiety," rather than pleasure, or relief, comes about when, instead of being gratified, an infant has an experience of being "not-gratified," and gradually comes to experience more complex negative or ambivalent *moments*, perhaps leading him to anticipate with anxiety instead of either frank pleasure or frank pain. We observe that some children develop more than a little anticipatory anxiety in advance of any transitions; others develop anticipatory anxiety in advance of only particular changes, not unlike an adult who has developed a phobia about getting on an airplane or taking an exam. In the population under consideration in this monograph, however, we often find a *lack* of anticipatory ability and appropriate use of anticipatory anxiety, i.e. not having sufficient pattern recognition to know when a change is about to take place, a part of their neurofunctional deficit that interferes with this aspect of processing everyday experiences.

Dr. Fallon's formulation that a child approaching a developmental reorganization, i.e. on the brink of "chaos," seems to me equivalent to formulating that a child in the throes of incipient developmental disorganization is experiencing a specific kind of signal anxiety, namely anticipatory anxiety. One could then make the argument that Dr. Fallon's theory is consistent with our observations of children showing anticipatory anxiety as they prepare for the next step, mustering one's ego apparatus to reorganize and restructure appropriately to the new situation. This is, of course, the role parents take in caring for their infants. Over the course of development, a child increasingly takes over by developing his own strategies.

Using Anna as an example, her deficit in transitioning was expressed in multiple ways, such as her refusal to get into her bed because she could not *know* where she would wake up; in her reacting to any new situation or person as if she were totally overwhelmed; and in her inability to tolerate making plans for vacations from therapy. All such transitions apparently left her feeling literally stranded—frozen, afraid, and defaulting into tantrums, avoidant behavior, or worse. In her play, we could see multiple aspects of her trying to conquer her anxiety about transitions: "going through the doorway" and repeatedly asking "what's on the other side" were regular themes. As she worked through this issue in her treatment, she showed the ability to anticipate and to manage change by playing at asking me to accompany her on her vacation, and showed that she could cope with the impending separation by making transitions at home and at school without falling apart.

Nonetheless, well into treatment she still showed the extent to which change made her angry and afraid of confiding in me, for fear that I would behave monstrously toward her. In her play, we enacted how "the monster" could also include the "suddenness" of a change, in that she played that the monster *came out of the blue*, literally representing her experience of a transition—without the ability to anticipate, she felt irrevocably controlled by anything or anyone who had an expectation of her that she couldn't meet, in the face of which she felt utterly helpless.

Another sign of Anna's growth was her evolving play about the details of going to sleep, anticipating the changes at bedtime and her fear of the "monster" by *rehearsing the known* to protect against the unknown.

JAY: UNDERSTANDING AN ADOLESCENT ON THE VERGE OF "CHAOS"

Understanding the role of anticipatory ability and anxiety in development seems highly relevant to making sense of the experience of Jay upon his becoming psychotic in his adolescence. It would appear that he was flooded with anxiety so overwhelming that he experienced a disconnect in his neurobiological functioning, a manifest expression of the alterations in the function of neurotransmitters at the cellular level that are involved in a psychotic breakdown. Whether one perceives psychosis in an adolescent as a consequence of a loss of parental structuring as a matter of development, as Dr. Fallon explains Jay's breakdown, or whether one perceives psychosis as a manifestation of a genetic or epigenetic neurophysiological shift at the level of neurotransmitters, as I do, the experience from the perspective of an adolescent confronting disorganization in mental structuring would be manifestly the same.

For a psychotic adolescent like Jay, not unlike an ASD child, the "moment" is described as one of displeasure, akin to anticipatory anxiety unconsciously linked to potential chaos, an unpleasurable feeling of being on the brink of the unknowable, neurobiologically lacking a mental roadmap for the next step. Neurobiologically, Jay was unable to call upon his ego apparatus to master sudden disorganization, unable to muster that mixture of thoughts, feelings, and prior experiences that help organize a new emotional/cognitive demand; the transition must have been experienced as a series of disconnections. Similar to the experience of an ASD child, Jay at the moment of his breakdown had lost his ability to organize symbol and affect so that they could be used for managing actions and relationships.

Therapy with Jay was similar to working with a child with ASD. Becoming psychotic likely feels like being autistic: words have no meaning, and cannot be used to organize thoughts and feelings. Thoughts themselves can be random, like so many pieces of a puzzle that make sense neither to the subject nor to the people trying to help. Jay, like an ASD child, behaved as though he lacked understanding of his own mental states and those of others, unable to integrate internal and external experiences, and he lacked the facility of expression, whether verbal or gestural, which would have made it possible to understand him.

Because of such deficits, one observes that, like an ASD child, the ego structure in someone who is in a psychotic state seems to compensate by acquiring a repertoire of defensive mechanisms that are inconsistent with flexible adaptations. Falling back on rigid defenses makes shifts to "organized conversation," i.e. therapeutic intervention or normal daily conversations, very difficult. The goal of an analyst with a psychotic adolescent can be similar to working with a child such as Evan: to reattach words to feelings, to label simple constructions before trying to label those more complex. The process of re-labeling helps regain the lost connections that are not only psychological but also neurobiological.

We often use jigsaw puzzles as metaphors for the work we do in psychoanalysis. Using such a template for understanding brain functioning, we would need a three-dimensional puzzle to picture the multiple ways the pieces connect for the developing baby. At the very least, an analytic technique with a child such as Evan or with a psychotic adolescent like Jay relies on knowing that from the outset, infants have an inborn mechanism for socialization, a strong urge to communicate both visually and verbally with others, and equally have a desire to understand other people's communications. Our technique relies upon the fact that children evolve increasingly complex skills in understanding their own and others' behavior, thoughts, and feelings, and they make meaning of the world of feelings attached to symbols, both in play and in language. The formation of an internal structure, the multi-dimensional network of brain activity, is not "experienced" but serves as implicit, scaffolded connections between body, mind, and emotion, influencing and influenced by interpersonal relationships over time. This construction is experienced in the treatment setting; with a child, the transference is mixed with concrete realities of the therapist-child relationship.

Working with Jay gave his analyst access to a picture of the massive chaos in the brain's networking activity that results from disorganization of a previously functioning neural structure—the multi-dimensional pieces of the puzzle—under the conditions of sudden physical and/or psychic trauma. Similarly, in working with Evan, his analyst sees a not dissimilar picture of the puzzle, but one caused by a brain that has genetically been programmed to have difficulty in forging the organization of the pieces from the outset of development.

UNDERSTANDING THE *MOMENT*

As psychoanalysts, we can turn to our models of neurodevelopmental processes—affect, cognition, and interpersonal experience—to try to inform our understanding of the *moment* that Dr. Fallon describes. His construct seems to refer to that essential bridge between affect and cognition that, by adolescence, one comes to expect to be on automatic pilot. In other words, when faced with a difficult situation, like leaving home or breaking up with a girlfriend, we rely on the structures that have gradually built up neurophysiologically to support negative emotions, trauma, or anxiety. In a negative "moment," anticipatory anxiety fails to be useful in either accessing language or calling upon a relationship to intervene and provide the needed support or rescue. Instead, psychotic anxiety, like the functioning of an ASD brain, destabilizes the organization of the brain, disrupts the tracks, overloads the signaling function, and leads to a sense of chaos. One suddenly seems to lose access to coping skills, especially cognitive functions which are essential to making meaning of one's experience.

In children with autistic spectrum disorder, development is altered by a neurobiological difference that leads to symptoms or behavioral differences. Dr. Fallon suggests that in an incipient psychosis, when on the brink of "chaos," the connections between affect, cognition, and memory of attachment experiences similarly evaporate. Without those connections, in the psychotic state, an adolescent like Jay shows alterations in his ability to engage in normal emotional relationships, struggles to communicate effectively, and suddenly lacks the ability for self and affect regulation. This alteration of ability to self-regulate in a child with uneven development, like Evan, leads to maladaptive behaviors, such as perseverative or ritualistic actions in play, as well as social withdrawal and avoidance, and overall rigidity alternating with intense displays of emotion difficult for a parent to modulate. Both Evan and Jay overreacted to sensory stimulation, as if failing to differentiate between those that were noxious and those that were benign.

In summary, psychoanalysis can serve to alter the neurobiological patterns in the brain: to connect, or reconnect parts of the brain that allow us to find meaning in feelings, thoughts, actions, and intentions, and to negotiate the stresses of internal and external experience. In children and adolescents, implicitly rewiring or enabling shifts in neurobiological patterns can allow for growth of or a return to normative ways of meeting developmental challenges. Dr. Fallon's formulation of the *moment*, thinking in terms of being on the brink of chaos when confronted with disorganizing, unprocessed affect, offers a way to think about the central task of analysis.

Chapter Five

Brief Notes from Three Clinical Cases

In this chapter, I aim to demonstrate the *moment* and how one might use this concept to work clinically using three additional cases as examples. For the sake of brevity, I have not tried to present entire cases, but rather a particular *moment* in the analysis and in the maturation of these individuals.

Thus far in this monograph, the psychoanalytic clinical material presented has been "extreme": psychosis in an adolescent and a toddler with early regulation and socialization difficulties. These "extreme" cases have been used to put in bold relief the *moment*, just as pathology in medicine has been used to explore normal development. With this "extreme" material presented thus far, a question arises as to whether the *moment* occurs in other circumstances including normal functioning. I asserted in Chapter 1 that the *moment* applies to extreme situations such as psychosis, autistic spectrum and trauma phenomena as well as to everyday development. The three cases presented in this chapter demonstrate the *moment* in more normative development.

Affect is a key component in understanding the concept of the *moment* in development. In Chapter 3, I explicated the vicissitudes of affect in the *moment* using our well studied understanding of the vicissitudes of affect in trauma. In addition, with the definition of affect provided in Chapter 3, I compare its role in the treatment of trauma with its role in the *moment*. In this chapter, I will present a case of an adolescent, Lilly, in which trauma occurred. This case demonstrates the clinical usefulness of the concept of the *moment* in freeing-up the process of development.

In the second case, I present notes from the analysis of an adult, Alice, who suffered trauma as an adolescent, similar to Lilly's. In this case, the overwhelming affect was sequestered using obsessional defenses, leaving the affect unmetabolized. As the analysis uncovered the affect, disorganization became apparent as the affect was experienced, tolerated and metabolized.

Once the unprocessed affect was uncovered and metabolized, Alice moved forward in her development in ways she had not been able to do prior to the analysis.

For the third case I present in this chapter, Mary, my intent is to show the usefulness of the concept of the *moment* in moving development along in a very different way. In this case, the child stalled in development because of a constitutional problem present from birth. This is a very different reason than in all of the other cases presented in this monograph. The presenting symptoms were a disconnected child who seemed to have no internal push of her own to drive her development forward.

In these three cases I demonstrate the concepts of affect and attachment that I have defined, as well as the idea of disorganization/reorganization in a super-ordinate line of development. Clinically, tracking the affect, and determining the limits of affect tolerance and the organizational capacity in these cases allowed me as the analyst to develop the attachment and choose when and how to help modulate affect and lend organizational capacities in the developmental process.

THE CASE OF LILLY

Lilly presented to me as a 15 year old in a very disorganized state, completely unable to function in school even to the point of not doing homework, not participating in classes, and not taking tests. She would go to class but when there, would lay her head on her desk and not participate. If anyone attempted to question her, she would yell at them to let her be. At home, she isolated herself in her room. If her family attempted to engage her, she would complain loudly that she could not tolerate the household and her father's rules. This would be followed by demands for autonomy, although it was clear that she had no idea how to carry out that autonomy.

The previous spring Lilly had been the lead in the school play. Three months prior to her entry into treatment, in September, she began school as a straight "A" student, was adored by peers and teachers alike and was in the process of writing a play. However, in the midst of all her successes, Lilly and her mother had been having more and more arguments which had been increasing in intensity. Finally at the beginning of October, Lilly and her mother had the most intense argument, their last one. After the argument, her mother left the house and drove away in a rage. Sometime that evening the family was notified that her mother had died in a car accident. Within days, things began to fall apart for Lilly. In the analytic work, just as in school, she was unable to tolerate any attempts to interact with her.

On presentation, her father told me the story of the mother's death and seemed profoundly aware of the *moment* and the devastating trauma to Lilly, although he could not tell me much about his daughter's development as her mother had done most of the child care. He had been deeply involved in his work. So with little understanding of Lilly's development, I began our work. As the work proceeded, I gradually uncovered the *moment* and recognized that it resonated throughout her development and was contained in the trauma.

Because of the nature of trauma and of development, and the way they collided for Lilly, it took some time for us to find a way to understand this *moment*. After that, there was some additional time to gather the data. But once the data was gathered and organized, it had an immediate effect. In addition to the organizational aspect, she had overwhelming affect involved that had to be modulated to a tolerable level, taking additional time. After both of these tasks were completed, she resumed her development.

At the core of Lilly's *moment* was a striving for autonomy. As best I could tell, this began when she was eighteen months old in her struggle to declare herself in the face of a mother who was challenged by such audacity. Although Lilly seemed to have made moderate protests, she reached latency with enough internal resources to become a compliant school age child who did well academically. But when pre-adolescence arrived, the conflicts resumed with a crescendo. With the death of her mother, this new piece of reality and the developmental challenge of autonomy had to be faced. However, the intensity of the affect was too great, the puzzle was one that had never been assembled, even in its simpler form when she was a toddler, and her organizational capacities were overwhelmed despite her intelligence.

The technical challenge for me as the analyst was in finding a way for Lilly to attach. She was frightened that her hate had killed her mother to whom she was profoundly, albeit ambivalently, attached. In order to protect me, she refused to talk with me. Day after day, Lilly sat in my office in silence with her back to me in a remote part of my consulting room. Sometimes she would allow me to speak, sometimes she would put on headphones and turn up the volume of her music to drown out whatever I might say. If I mentioned her mother, her history or her current situation, she would shout, "stay out of my business." Any attempt on my part to be empathic would be met with "shut up" and Lilly holding her ears. She did, however, come to my office promptly for every session with little objection.

After a difficult initial period of three months, Lilly did find ways acceptable to her to attach to me. The first was that she found an email correspondent who lived several states away. For a few months, after each of our sessions, she went home and emailed this correspondent. Presumably, the contents of the emails had to do with her thoughts and feelings experienced in our session. Somewhat later, she set up an online blog and recorded her reactions to our sessions on a public forum.

Despite her wish to make contact with me, she was also determined to protect me from what I suspected were hateful and disorganized thoughts and feelings. I never saw these entries and when I found out about the public online blóg, I wondered with her if she wanted me to see what she was writing. I was told that she left the office that day and immediately removed all of her entries from the blog.

After about 6 months into our analytic work, Lilly did begin communicating with me by telling her father about our sessions and the father would then regularly tell me what she had said. I would let her know what her father had told me and my thoughts about her comments. Then, in a day or two I would hear back from the father about her reactions. And so it continued.

In this manner, it became obvious that she had not been able to construct a narrative of what had happened between her and her mother. For her, there was no meaning to the events, only overwhelming feelings. In fact, up to that time, no one seemed to have a narrative that gave meaning to her actions. Thereafter, for a number of sessions, in her presence, I called everyone who could tell me about her and her mother. I did this on speaker phone so she could hear. One of her relatives found journal material that her mother had written when Lilly was a toddler. I read it aloud to her in the office. With my phone calls, reading and commentary, Lilly sat quietly and listened. As we gathered and compiled this information from all of her relatives, it felt as if both Lilly and I together were constructing a meaningful narrative of the trauma, but also of her life. She was passive, but now she was listening for the first time with me.

Finally, I wrote three paragraphs that noted Lilly and her mother's struggle in trying to find a way to be with each other, starting as a toddler and on in to early adolescence. I pointed to the uncomfortable feelings of hate that the struggle generated. Then with her mother's death, I imagined that Lilly's overwhelming feelings made it impossible for her to sort out everything that happened, despite her strong wish to find her own solutions, independent of others.

When I gave Lilly this narrative, she accepted it and took it home. When I asked her about it a few sessions later, she began yelling that I should get away from her. As I was almost as far away from her in the room as I could be, I continued to sit where I was and look at her. She then yelled that I should stop looking at her, saying that she would leave if I did not. She began to walk toward me. I reflexively stood up. She leaned back, gathered saliva in her mouth, and spit, just missing my face. She then ran out of the office.

Within 45 seconds, there was a phone call. I answered it. There was complete silence at the other end of the telephone. I asked if this was Lilly. Still silence. I said I was "okay." I then heard a sigh. I asked if she was okay. The phone disconnected. In answer to my question, her stepmother called me a minute later to let me know that Lilly had informed her of what had happened and that Lilly was okay.

Although it was never confirmed, I understood this event to be a re-enactment of the last argument that Lilly and her mother had. We both had experienced her *moment* and brought it to life just as a play does. The next day, Lilly came in and took her usual place at the far end of my office. I thanked her for letting me know that she was okay after leaving yesterday.

It had been almost 7 months since we began our work and her presence in school had been getting more difficult for her teachers and peers. Within less than a week after the completed narrative and re-enactment, she and her teachers had determined what she needed to do to complete her present grade. She suddenly began to do her school work. Within two months, she had completed all the work that was required for the year and graduated to the next grade.

Lilly's struggle for autonomy and her mother's difficulty in being able to help her, along with the jarring trauma in which Lilly both completely lost her attachment and felt responsible for its destruction caused her developmental *moment* to hang in a metastable state. In this *moment*, the overwhelming affect came both from the hate that was generated in being frustrated in her bids for autonomy as well as the anguish at having lost her mother. She was unable to back away from her *moment* through compliance as she had done in latency.

Let us enumerate the elements of Lilly's *moment*:

- The pressure of her striving for autonomy
- The overwhelming affect coming from several sources
- The hate that had been generated by her frustration in her striving for autonomy
- The sadness and loss of her attachment, her mother
- Her sense of responsibility for her mother's death and her terror that her hate might have done this
- Her loss of her attachment (as I have defined it in Chapter 4)
- The disorganization of her model of the world. This disorganization was reflected in her inability to emotionally know where she had come from, or where she was going. In essence, she had no meaning in life. For example, how was she to mourn her mother?

The inner push to move on in development, with the inability to do so which was fueled by anxiety and disorganization, led to a downward spiral ending in a complete breakdown of ego functions. She was unable to organize her memories into a coherent narrative that gave meaning to the state in which she now lived. Although we would not say she was psychotic, she constructed an unsustainable model of the world in which she saw herself as already autonomous. In that unsustainable model, she did not see any need for an attachment.

The analytic work helped her construct a meaningful, albeit painful narrative. The greatest technical challenge in this case was finding a way for Lilly to have an attachment without having to acknowledge it. This was difficult because of Lilly's aversion to any attachment, given the ambivalent one that she had with her mother, and the sense that her own affect felt so toxic to herself and to others (recall Jay's fear that his music would infect others). With the *moment* processed and the developmental challenge met, Lilly was able to move on, which happened almost immediately.

There is, of course, more to this story, but this one piece of it is an illustration of the usefulness of understanding and working with the *moment* in development and in psychoanalytic work.

THE CASE OF ALICE

The second case which I will very briefly present here is again an example of a *moment* in the context of trauma. Alice was a middle-aged woman who presented for analysis with difficulty being productive in any career. She was bright, capable and accomplished such that she had begun several promising careers including real estate agent, a college professor, and a psychotherapist, only to lose interest.

Her history included the death of both of her parents, both from illnesses that lasted only weeks before they died. Her mother died when Alice was in early adolescence and her father died four years later. After the death of her mother, she developed religious rituals that consumed a considerable amount of time, although she hid the rituals from everyone. She also focused on becoming an excellent student, whereas before her mother's death she had been a mediocre student. In the initial interviews and even for much of the treatment, she reported that she remembered nothing around the time of her mother's death, and yet she reported many details. There was, however, a strong sense of not knowing.

In the early part of treatment, she focused on her present life and in the course of that work, she began to focus on writing which she had always loved. An anxiety that kept appearing in her associations as well as her writing had its origins around a sense of disorganization. It took some time before she could tolerate the direct experience and was able to talk about it. As the analysis progressed, her writing converged on her life growing up. In the course of her writing, when she approached material around the trauma of the loss of her parents, her writing would become disorganized and chaotic even to the point of her not being able to physically write words on a page.

As the analysis progressed, she was able to tolerate more and more strong affect as well as feelings of disorganization and not knowing. With this, she was able to write material that she quickly got published.

As we got closer to the affect associated with her mother's death, she began experiencing episodes of depersonalization, derealization and disorientation. For example, while driving, she would suddenly not know where she was, where she was coming from or going to. It became clear that the obsessional symptoms that had developed shortly after her mother's death had contained the intolerable affect which had occurred with her at the time of her mother's death but could only be accessed through bodily sensations. Rather than anything repressed, it was clear that these affects had never been experienced in the sense of a known experience. As only bodily sensations but without meaning, Alice recognized that in this state she did not "know" that her mother was gone (Fernando, 2012). Language here is difficult to convey the experience; nonetheless, her experiences match the descriptions given by Bollas (1987) as "thought unknown." As we got to this material and she was able to tolerate it, then put a narrative to it, she became more invested in her writing which blossomed. With this, she was able to experience the chaotic, creative thought processes in her writing, just as she was able to allow it in thinking about her past and present life experiences—and just as Jay had done with his music.

In the case of Alice who suffered the loss of her parents in adolescence, she contained the affects in an unmetabolized state using her obsessions and compulsions. Because she was unable to tolerate its disorganizing effects, she was unable to metabolize it without an attachment to me, the analyst. I helped her modulate the affect and think about the experience. In the analytic process as she allowed herself to experience the affect, the disorganizing effects were revealed. With continued analysis, she was able to process the affect (as seen in her writing) and create new organizational processes that allowed her to finally meet her developmental challenges, move on and choose a career which in this case became writing.

THE CASE OF MARY

In the exploration of the *moment* in chapter 3, I remarked that development will not move forward if the affect is too intense, leading to disorganization. I also mentioned that development may not move forward if there is too little affect. Mary, the third example of the *moment* in this chapter, is a case of too little affect. In fact, the beginning of the work with this child was a search for a source of affect.

Mary, the oldest of three, was born with cerebral palsy and without a corpus callosum. The corpus callosum is a structure that connects the right side of the brain with the left side of the brain and allows these two sides to communicate with each other. At age 12, although she was enrolled in school and even had an eighth grade reading ability, Mary would sit in a room alone and play the same segment of classical music over and over again. She had the ability to listen to a piece of music and could then play the melody on the piano. Despite her spastic fine motor difficulties, when she played on a musical keyboard, her movements were steady and firm. She also would sometimes type on a keyboard/computer, although she would not share what she had written with anyone.

Her mother described Mary as having no expressed affect. Much later in our work together, but long before we were finished, there was a discussion about anger in Mary's classroom. After 45 minutes of silent listening, Mary raised her hand and said with some firmness that she had never experienced anger in her life. In the initial interview, Mary sat beside her mother motionless and without apparent affect for the entire session. There was no effort to touch her mother or rub up against her. After 40 minutes or so, I turned to Mary and asked a simple question that I thought she could easily answer. How old was she?

There was absolutely no response, verbal or non-verbal. In fact, I was not sure that Mary even heard the question. After about 2 minutes of waiting in silence, I abandoned the quest and turned back to talk with her mother. About 2 minutes after that, suddenly the word "twelve" came from a place in the room that was hard to locate. I had not been patient enough.

As I began to meet with Mary regularly, I knew that she could be engaged but wondered how to do that. After various attempts, including trying to have a conversation, presenting sundry toys, waiting in silence for some spontaneous production, and playing music, I sat her down in front of my keyboard/computer and typed a question. "How are you?" "Fine," was the answer that appeared on the screen despite her spastic fine motor activity.

With this medium, I began to ask her about her response to the world in as many ways as I could imagine. I got the same response, "Fine." After a while I discovered that she watched a reality TV show, *The Weakest Link*, a sequel to an earlier reality TV show, *Survivor*, in which seven people were challenged to survive on a desert island. In *The Weakest Link*, each week the person least likely to survive was kicked off the island and a newcomer joined.

Soon we were reproducing the program using the computer keyboard as our medium of communication. There was no response to me as a person, but she would reliably respond to every one of my keyboard inputs. She would spontaneously and without hesitation type what she was thinking. What she was thinking was that I was the weakest link and she told me so. After a time, she began to demand that I do the walk of shame, a ritual done by the person leaving the island.

As I tried to understand and explore the motive behind her interests, I asked various questions. Each question was rebuffed with, "Just do the walk of shame." With my persistent questions, she finally came back with a novel response, "Bank it. Just do the walk of shame." "Bank it?" I replied. "Quit belly-aching and just do the walk of shame." "That's funny," I wrote.

It was funny. "Bank it?" "Quit belly-aching?" Here we were sitting next to each other, each seemingly anonymously typing on the same keyboard. She continued to be expressionless in countenance and non-verbal. But the screen revealed a very different story, a repartee of two people bumping up against one another, shoving each other in what felt like a light-hearted way.

I finally acquiesced and did the walk of shame. But before I signed off that show, I proclaimed that I was now going to migrate to another TV show, *Queen for a Day*. She wanted to come too. And so we began to explore what made her feel like a queen. The answer was simple, a coke and a piece of pizza, just like when she went out with her dad to the local pizza place.

We had now clarified two pieces of her puzzle: what she liked and what she did not like. With those pieces firmly in place, we moved closer to the real world. We moved to the doll house and began using real figures.

For my work with Mary at that point, humor was an extremely valuable tool. Most of the time she was expressionless in countenance as well as verbally. When I would hit upon something that had an affective charge to it, she would laugh with glee, even from the very beginning. For example, Mary had mentioned her dog at one point in our game show work. With that, I discovered that whenever I picked up the dog figure, she laughed with glee.

I soon discovered that it was even funnier if the dog began to push objects and even more so, people around. By closer and closer approximation, I discovered that kicking the baby out of the cradle elicited the most affect. Then I hypothesized that it was really that she wanted to kick her two younger brothers out of the cradle, and then occupy the cradle herself. Yes, that brought even more glee.

Gradually we began to put together various pieces brought along by their affective elements, and after a couple of years we had organized and assembled a picture of at least a portion of her world and her narrative. As the oldest of three, her brothers were superseding her. In addition, she felt resentful that she had been displaced as the baby by her younger siblings who were 4 and 6 years younger than her.

Once this story was assembled with all of the affective elements, she took delight in it as we re-enacted it in the dollhouse. She was comfortable with her anger, that was now represented by a Tyrannosaurus rex. To this dear pet she gave the name of the boisterous owner of her favorite pizza joint. When this anger was aroused, she had no problem sweeping everything away, especially all the other babies, with his powerful tail, laughing with glee. After a relatively short period, we moved on to the next *moment*, although we would occasionally revisit this one, especially when something in her environment challenged her, such as negotiating with a new roommate.

As our work progressed, she became more verbal, more aware of her wants and desires and more expressive of them. And with this, development was unleashed and progressed as she became more aware of the world and cultivated more interests. She began socializing with peers. Although there continued to be a delay between a stimulus and her affective response and her range of emotions was not as full and nuanced as her age-mates, this delay reduced from four minutes to less than 20 seconds, and her range of emotions had increased from nothing to glee at aggression. Soon in our play she became the principal of the school and I became her secretary and servant, while she ordered me about.

This case illustrates development from a *moment* in which there was not enough affective fuel to motivate the process. With support from the treatment, development happened and it is unlikely that the neurobiology of an absent corpus callosum changed anatomically. Given a neurobiological perspective, one could speculate that there were nerve pathways that grew, allowing the mind to develop. Perhaps one day with technology that does not exist today, we may be able to visualize these novel pathways. If they can be shown, we may be able to show that these pathways developed as a result of the analytic work that was done.

In the meantime, what can be seen in the present, without invoking neurobiology and some future technology, is that the mind changed. The mind developed and matured. In this case, mediated by attachment, the analyst lent both the emotional fuel and the organizational capacities to move development forward. The developmental process helped Mary build a reasonably working internal model of the world. Equipped with this model, she could then move through her world with purpose rather than just sitting alone, stalled in development, listening to the same music over and over. Again, this was done by tracking the affect, initially primarily conveyed by laughing and humor. As best I was able to determine, there was no disruption of Mary's cognitive or organizational capacities by overwhelming affect. However, demonstrating a higher level of organization, her spastic motor activity lessened as our work progressed. I take this as a bodily sign of her more organized mind. When we did find the affect, it was full of gusto, like a breath of fresh air.

Chapter Six

Summary, Comments, Implications and Open Questions

We have come to the end of my explication of the *moment*, although there is much more to understand and explore in this concept. For me, this exploration has illuminated my understanding and practice of psychoanalysis in the way subatomic physics explicates molecular physics. It goes below the surface and illuminates the mechanisms of processes and dictums of psychoanalysis.

For example, it gives us an understanding of what is meant by timing of an interpretation, and even where interpretation fits into development and maturation. It gives us a glimpse of the process of intergenerational transmission of organizational processes. It illuminates and explicates affect and attachment. The concept of the *moment* also provides a more explicit mechanism of defense analysis. It may even provide some insight as to why the brilliant man who first clarified defense interpretation ended the last year of his life in prison in one of the freest countries in the world. I will discuss these implications toward the end of this chapter.

I begin this chapter with a summary of what I have formulated in this monograph regarding the *moment*. No doubt there will be many who do not acccpt my formulation. I believe, however, that if one can acknowledge the material with skepticism if not curiosity, then there are some conclusions and implications of the *moment* to our understanding of psychological development and psychoanalysis. I will review conclusions, and finally I will raise some questions regarding the concept of the *moment* and its implications.

SUMMARY

I began this monograph describing the concept of the *moment* in which the individual is on the verge of moving to the next level of development. To illustrate this, I used cases in which the individual was in chaos. The individuals in conjunction with their environments and their attachment figures were not able to move themselves to the next level of maturity. In the psychoanalytic process, that forward movement was facilitated and could be observed.

These cases demonstrated that the leading edge of development is that *moment* in the process when new material is discovered, rendering what the individual knew before as obsolete. In order for the individual to move on in development, the model of the world which is in disarray due to the newly discovered material, must be taken down, revised, and then reinstated in its new iteration. The process is moved along by an inner push for development and by the organizational processes that have been embedded in the person through previous episodes of development. The capacity to organize itself is revised and improved. This process of organizing the organizing process itself (what has been called self-organizing systems) led me, in chapter 3, to discuss organizational capacity as a super-ordinate line of development. With a new, organized and improved model of the world that incorporates the newly discovered material and new and improved ways of organizing the world, the individual can then proceed in life with a model of reality that more closely matches what one can expect to encounter in life.

In the *moment*, the organizational capacity itself is being reorganized, leaving the developing person vulnerable to disorganization. The individual's ability to tolerate the affect and specifically anxiety that accompanies the uncertainty of a not-yet-known model is an important component, particularly in relation to resisting cognitive disruption which leads to further disorganization. When the level of affect gets too high and the cognitive capacities and ability to organize degrade to the point that there begins to be a positive feedback loop and a downward spiral, an individual's attachment becomes critical.

The role of attachment is to modulate affect and lend organizational capacities to the individual. A significant aspect of the attachment is the individual's ability to call in and use those attachments. The helper, as I will call it here, the one providing the attachment, usually but certainly not limited to a therapist or a parent, must be able to monitor the individual's level of affect, cognitive capacities, and the ability to organize. If the attachment is working, the individual will accept these supports from the helper.

Attachments buffer the disorganizing effects and assist with the organizing processes that are in play in the *moment*—keeping in mind that attachment at different developmental levels provides different supports, qualitatively and quantitatively. Those individuals whose attachments are compromised either because of abuse and neglect, or because of innate weaknesses such as those in the autistic spectrum, are in a vulnerable position when it comes to facing these *moments*. Similarly, psychological trauma and innate sensitivities challenge individuals and exacerbate the vulnerabilities on the "edge of chaos."

In this discussion it is important to acknowledge that the use of the terms *affect* and *attachment* here have been defined in particular ways that I discussed in chapter 3. It is also useful, in order to understand the dynamic nature of the *moment*, to consider what general complex non-linear systems theory has to say about evolving systems. That is, in the process of evolving, a system, such as the mind, must disorganize in order to reorganize. This occurs when the system is pushed to the edge of chaos. In the process of evolving, there is a risk of collapse to the system.

In what I will call normative development, this process of disorganization/reorganization takes place in small incremental steps that are barely noticeable, and is shepherded by good enough attachments. It does not usually involve dramatic spirals into chaos, although if you look closely, you will see minor slippage of cognitive processes even in normative development. For example, slippage is readily noticeable in many toddlers during potty training when the child's language abilities momentarily slip. Similarly, in the course of routine psychoanalysis, I see, or sometimes even my analysands call my attention to moments of confusion when they are on the verge of coming to a new level of understanding of themselves or of the world.

For example, one adult analysand of mine noted that she felt like she was trying to navigate a new world and needed a GPS (global positioning system) but did not have one. Another one of my patients who had written a book said that he would struggle sometimes for months with each chapter, writing and re-writing. Then suddenly one day it would all be clear and he would write it in an almost finished form from beginning to end in one sitting. In thinking about the developmental line of organizational processes, as a matter of course in everyone's development, one would expect to see small incremental challenges to organization which would lead to incremental compensation and then development of new capacities of the mind to organize, without a load of drama. The concept of the *moment* can cue us in to these subtle incremental changes.

The concept of the *moment* also predicts situations and circumstances when the process is likely to be more cataclysmic. Examples of those situations have been provided in the clinical cases in this monograph. The case of Evan provided an example of when a person's constitution or development makes it difficult to accept support from an attachment figure. The lack of attachment figures also creates a vulnerable situation which, as in the case of Lilly, can occur when a parent dies. Lilly and Alice are also case examples of trauma when the unprocessed affect is too high, another impediment to moving through the *moment*. Increased sensitivities such as with Evan also put individuals at more risk of being overwhelmed by affect.

In some situations, the developmental challenge is too great. For example, in the case of Jay, his early identification with his homosexual father clashed with his own heterosexual strivings to create unprocessed, and for him, unprocessible affect that was brought to the fore with an intense (and what would ordinarily have been a normative) sexual relationship in an expected developmental *moment* for a late adolescent. Because Jay was unable to contain the *moment* and there was no one to assist, disorganization led to further disorganization which finally led to complete collapse of the ego. Mary, on the other hand, demonstrated a circumstance in which there was not enough affect constitutionally to push the developmental process along.

Another significant aspect that can create difficulties is a mismatch between the attachment figure and the developmental need of the maturing individual. In early childhood, the child is materially dependent on the parent for survival and has little choice in accepting support from the attachment figure. In the case of Evan, and also in the early development of Lilly, the parent's presence most of the time prevailed in preventing the child from completely devolving into chaos, although the parents could not assist enough to move development forward.

During adolescence, however, when there is an inner push for autonomy, the parent's support is not as easily taken in. Adolescence is also a time when the intensity of feelings, particularly sexual and aggressive feelings, increase due to sex hormones and upsurge of the drives. This increased affect makes adolescents more vulnerable to disorganization. This example was illustrated by the case of both Jay and Lilly. It is likely for this reason that the psychoses, schizophrenia and mania, present in adolescence and young adulthood.

COMMENTS AND IMPLICATIONS

At this point, I would like to make a few comments about the concept of the *moment* and spell out some implications for our understanding of development and of psychoanalysis. I hope I have demonstrated to the reader that conceptualizing the *moment* and a super-ordinate organizational line of development is useful in evaluating development and in navigating the therapeutic process, particularly in vulnerable individuals. In this monograph I have addressed psychoanalytic work in contrast to the more general psychotherapeutic work because what is characteristic of unprocessed affect is that it is experienced but has no meaning.

This is where more superficial psychotherapies fail. The disorganization/reorganization process must be recognized as a lived experience. One aspect of that lived experience, one that directly involves the therapist and his participation in the treatment is what we might refer to as transference, although the experience is broader than just transference.

In fact, if the analyst can conceptualize and work with the analysand's experience of unprocessed affect and the properties of the *moment*, the analyst can more easily help the analysand recognize the nature of the experience. In this manner, the analysand's experienced transference can be more easily disconnected from the analyst, enabling the analyst to work more as an ally and a partner. I have used the term *attachment* and the role of attachment to describe this process.

A key to understanding the anatomy of the *moment* is unprocessed affect and unprocessed sense perceptions. All of us have experienced unprocessed affect. By its very nature, however, it can only be recalled as bodily sensations that have no words, no meaning. It is not like a memory of a known experience that has been repressed. It has never been organized into a meaningful experience. It is only bodily sensations without organization. This state is dysphoric and pushes us to quickly make a known experience out of it, to metabolize the affect and organize the sense perceptions into a meaningful experience.

The *moment* of taking in the unprocessed affect and sense perceptions is ubiquitous in human existence, and yet is very dysphoric. The combination of the dysphoria and the manner of recall as only a bodily experience without meaning or words has allowed the process to remain unnoticed despite its being so ubiquitous and in plain view. Being able to hold a *moment* and observe it might be akin to holding fire. Once you have that perspective, you know what to look for, how to organize the data and the processes. Becoming aware of a *moment* is likely to be a key to understanding the developmental challenges on which many of our analysands have gotten stuck and why they present to us for help. We can use our understanding of this state to help us in our analytic process by:

Knowing that we are in a *moment,* "on the edge of chaos" with a patient. This *moment* marks the spot of unprocessed affect and an experience waiting/wanting to be created. That spot is one from which we need to proceed even as we do not understand it and have no meaning attached to it.

When we are aware of the *moment* and understand what is happening, we as analysts can more easily withstand the disorganizing effect of the strong affect, and can more calmly begin to take stock of the situation, gather the data, look at the pieces, and begin the organizing process.

More effectively providing the support and the space needed for our patients to create and grow the organizing processes that will eventually contain and finally metabolize their unprocessed affect, allowing them to move on in their development.

Understanding the *moment* also has implications for what we know as defense analysis. William Reich (1933) predicated defense analysis on the idea that we put on character armor as a matter of some choice and perhaps even with some sly and cunning ability. The concept of the *moment* poses a different process. Instead of defenses being an ability, the concept of the *moment* suggests that defenses may be limitations. That is, when the *moment* cannot move forward, it is not because the individual has purposely and cunningly protected himself, but because the information could not be organized and the affect could not be metabolized. In the concept of the *moment*, it is the limitations of the mind that interfere with development. Defenses, then, can be conceptualized to be compensatory mechanisms that attempt to mitigate that downward spiral into chaos.

In this context, a defense is a cognitive slippage. Therefore, defenses are not something to be removed, but rather point to inabilities with which the individual needs assistance. For example, you would not think that an interpretation would have any effect on a cognitive slippage any more than you would think an interpretation would have an effect on mental retardation. Paul Gray's idea of close process monitoring (1994) moves us closer to the concept of the *moment* by monitoring the anxiety and watching the defense in action. But simply calling attention to this process, as Gray suggests, may not be sufficient. The individual may need additional assistance in modulating the affect and in organizing the material.

This is not to say that all defenses are of this character. I leave that as an open question. However, we know that the relentless attacking of defenses leaves anyone in a disorganized and even psychotic state, as demonstrated by the work of Habib Davenloo (1995). It might leave one to wonder if the person who wrote the book on defenses as character armor might not have brought himself to the same state of disorganization in his quest to understand himself by stripping away compensatory mechanism.

Likewise, the idea of interpretation by which one might mean confronting or by providing organization to material may not be enough for a psychoanalytic process to occur. The concept of the *moment* makes clear that attachment is necessary. In any effective psychoanalytic process, attachment is likely present. In the literature the word *alliance* has been used. In these discussions of alliance in the literature, however, there is little about lending of ego structure either in organizational function or in affect modulation. Therefore, we may need to rethink what is important and necessary for psychoanalytic process.

The ideas of lending ego capacity being a necessary part of the psychoanalytic process is a familiar one for most child psychoanalysts, but I suspect it leaves many adult-only psychoanalysts uncomfortable. And yet, I imagine that behind closed doors, effective adult analysts manage to provide these functions in the consulting room. The difficulty is to get more traditional analysts to admit this. Yet until we acknowledge what we actually do in the consulting room, we cannot even be respectful of our own work, let alone articulate it to the world. A key to this acknowledgment can be an understanding of the power and discomfort of unprocessed affect.

I want to add a footnote here about my own experience in being able to grasp and hold unprocessed affect. For me a key to being able to hold and appreciate the power of unprocessed affect has been what in the last 30 years has come to be called mindfulness and mindfulness meditation. The forced inactivity of meditation, just as with psychoanalysis but without the distraction of words and ideas, promotes a focus on the bodily experience. This experience in both formal and informal meditation, has been indispensable to me in my exploration of this work.

OPEN QUESTIONS

In my work here, I have left many questions unanswered. Some of these questions that interest me include the following:

If we consider the cases of Jay, Lilly, and Alice, we see a contrast between one adolescent who experienced hallucinations and delusions and two others who did not. One question is why are some individuals more prone to this phenomenon. All three of these individuals behaved irrationally and were disorganized. In fact, by my observation, being irrational and disorganized is quite common in the human condition. The more general and perhaps more significant question, it seems to me, is how it is that some individuals are able to contain the disorganization and irrationality. The concept of the *moment* does go a long way to understanding this question, but I think this question still stands, just as it does in all of medicine when one considers why some people get ill and others do not when exposed to the same noxious agent.

Another question that I believe my work has left is one regarding attachment. What is the nature of attachment and how does this attachment work? There are some possibilities posed in the literature. For example, Gergely (2007) has studied how parents modulate their infants' affects. There is however, much more to understand here. Since the action of attachment works in the face of inability to metabolize, process and organize, the mechanisms, modes and sites of action must be at a very basic functioning level.

In several places in this monograph, I have talked about an inner push that moves development along. Some of this inner push seems to be the dysphoria that unprocessed affect creates. Some of the inner push may be timed and seemingly inevitable preprogramed biological processes such as adrenarchy and puberty. Some of it may be increasing capacities of the brain brought about by myelination, for example. Spitz wrote about organizers (René Arpad Spitz & Cobliner, 1965), although it is not clear if he meant these organizers as happenings that create forward development, or if he just meant them to be markers of forward development. Nonetheless, I think there are many questions left unanswered regarding forces that move development forward.

Finally, I think there are still many questions about the nature of unprocessed sense perceptions, affect, and especially about unprocessed cognition that Varela (1991) raises. I believe these questions are ripening at this point in history. Psychoanalytic research, the kind I have demonstrated here as well as the more biological and measurement driven kind, has important contributions to make. Inasmuch as the field of psychoanalysis makes these contributions, it will reap benefits by increasing its effectiveness in understanding and helping improve the human condition.

References

Arieti, S. (1966). The Psychoanalytic Approach to the Psychoses. *Am. J. Psychoanal, 26*, 63–66.

Association, A. P., & Association, A. P. (1980). DSM-III: Diagnostic and Statistical Manual of Mental Disorders APA. *Washington, DC*, 205–225.

Bacciagaluppi, M. (2011). The Study of Psychic Trauma. *J. Amer. Acad. Psychoanal., 39*, 525–538.

Baron-Cohen, S., Leslie, A. M., & Frith, U. (1985). Does the autistic child have a "theory of mind"? *Cognition, 21*(1), 37–46. doi:10.1016/0010-0277(85)90022-8.

Benveniste, P. S., Papouchis, N., Allen, R., & Hurvich, M. (1998a). Rorschach Assessment of *Psychoanal. Psychol., 15*, 536–566.

Benveniste, P. S., Papouchis, N., Allen, R., & Hurvich, M. (1998b). Rorschach Assessment of Annihilation Anxiety and Ego Functioning. *Psychoanal. Psychol., 15*, 536–566.

Bertalanffy, L. von. (1952). *Problems of Life*. London: Watts.

Bion, W. R. (1962). *Learning from Experience*. London, UK: Tavistock.

Bion, W. R. (1963). *Elements of Psycho-Analysis*. London, UK: Heinemann.

Bion, W. R. (1965). *Transformations: Change from Learning to Growth*. London, UK: Tavistock.

Bollas, C. (1987). *The Shadow of the Object: Psychoanalysis of Unknown Thought*. Free Association Books.

Bowlby, J. (1969). *Attachment and Loss: Volume 1 Attachment* (Vol. 1). London: Penguin Group.

Chessick, R. D. (1995). Nothingness, Meaninglessness, Chaos, and the "Black Hole" Revisited. *J. Amer. Acad. Psychoanal., 23*, 581–601.

Davanloo, H. (1995). Intensive short-term psychotherapy with highly resistant patients. I. Handling resistance. In *Selected Papers of Habib Davanloo* (pp. 1–27). New York, NY: Wiley.

Demos, E. V. (2008). Basic Human Priorities Reconsidered. *Ann. Psychoanal., 36*, 246–265.

Dodds, J. (2011). *Psychoanalysis and ecology at the edge of chaos: complexity theory, Deleuze/Guattari and psychoanalysis for a climate in crisis*. London; New York: Routledge.

Erikson, E. H. (1956). The Problem of Ego Identity. *J. Amer. Psychoanal. Assn., 4*, 56–121.

Fernando, J. (2012). Trauma and the Zero Process. *Canadian J. Psychoanal., 20*, 267–290.

Fonagy, P., Gergely, G., Jurist, E., & Target, M. (2002). *Affect regulation, mentalization, and the development of the self.* New York: Other Press.

Freud, A. (1963). The concept of developmental lines. *The Psychoanalytic Study of the Child, 18*, 245–265.

Freud, S. (1923). The Ego and the Id, Volume XIX (1923-1925): *The Ego and the Id and Other Works*, 1-66, *XIX (1923-1925)*, 1–66.

Galatzer-Levy, R. M. (2002). Emergence. *Psychoanal. Inq.*, *22*, 708–727.

Galatzer-Levy, R. M. (2009). Finding Your Way Through Chaos, Fractals, and other Exotic Mathematical Objects: A Guide for the Perplexed. *J. Amer. Psychoanal. Assn.*, *57*, 1227–1249.

Garrett, M. (2012). Psychoanalysis and the Severely Mentally Ill. *The American Psychoanalyst*, *46*(1), 20 & 22.

Gergely, G. (1992). Developmental Reconstructions: Infancy from the Point of View of Psychoanalysis and Developmental Psychology. *Psychoanal. Contemp. Thought*, *15*, 3–55.

Gergely, G. (2007). The social construction of the subjective self: The role of affect-mirroring, markedness, and ostensive communication in self development. In L. C. Mayes, P. Fonagy, & M. Target (Eds.), *Developmental Science and Psychoanalysis*. London, UK: Karnac.

Gesell, A. (1925). *The Mental Growth of the Preschool Child*.

Ghent, E. (2002). Wish, Need, Drive: Motive in the Light of Dynamic Systems Theory and Edelman's Selectionist Theory. *Psychoanal. Dial.*, *12*, 763–808.

Gleick, J. (1987). *Chaos: Making a New Science*.

Gottschalk, L. A., Falloon, I. R. H., Marder, S. R., Lebell, M. B., Gift, T. E., & Wynne, L. C. (1988). The prediction of relapse of schizophrenic patients using emotional data obtained from their relatives. *Psychiatry Research*, *25*(3), 261–276. doi:10.1016/0165-1781(88)90097-2.

Gray, P. (1987). On the Technique of Analysis of the Superego—An Introduction. *Psychoanal Q*, *56*, 130–154.

Gray, Paul. (1994). *The Ego and Analysis of Defense*. London, UK: Jason Aronson.

Greenacre, P. (1975). On Reconstruction. *J. Amer. Psychoanal. Assn.*, *23*, 693–712.

Grotstein, J. S. (1990a). Nothingness, Meaninglessness, Chaos, and the "Black Hole" I—The Importance of Nothingness, Meaninglessness, and Chaos in Psychoanalysis 10. *Contemp. Psychoanal.*, *26*, 257–290.

Grotstein, J. S. (1990b). Nothingness, Meaninglessness, Chaos, and the "Black Hole" II—The Black Hole 12. *Contemp. Psychoanal.*, *26*, 377–407.

Grotstein, J. S. (1991). Nothingness, Meaninglessness, Chaos, and the "Black Hole" III—Self- and Interactional Regulation and the Background Presence of Primary Identification. *Contemp. Psychoanal.*, *27*, 1–33.

Hamburg, P. (1987). Symptoms, Chaos and the Architecture of Psychotherapy. *Mod. Psychoanal.*, *12*, 187–193.

Harry, H., & Stephen, S. (1970). Nature of Love: Simplified. *American Psychologist*, *25*(2), 161–168. doi:10.1037/h0029383.

Hurvich, M. S. (1989). Traumatic Moment, Basic Dangers and Annihilation Anxiety. *Psychoanal. Psychol.*, *6*, 309–323.

Jay. (2011). *The Life Replacement*. tfallon50@gmail.com. This audio recording can be obtained for a small fee from T. Fallon through email at tfallon50@gmail.com.

Johnson, M. (1987). *The body in the mind: The bodily basis of meaning, imagination, and reason*. Chicago, IL: University of Chicago Press.

Kaplan, S. (2002). Two boys — one event: How memories are recalled in interviews about massive trauma. *Scand. Psychoanal. Rev.*, *25*, 108–116.

Kieffer, C. C. (2007). Emergence and the Analytic Third: Working at the Edge of Chaos. *Psychoanal. Dial.*, *17*, 683–703.

Klein, M. (1975). *Envy and Gratitude and Other Works 1946–1963:* Edited by: M. Masud and R. Khan (Vol. 104). London, UK: The Hogarth Press and the Institute of Psychoanalysis.

Knafo, D. (2012). Working at the Limits of Human Experience. *The American Psychoanalyst*, *46*(2), 17–18, 20.

Kocan, M. (2012). Treating Patients Vulnerable to Psychotic Regression. *The American Psychoanalyst*, *46*(1), 21–22.

Koehler, B. (2011). Psychotic Disorders: From DNA to Neighborhood. *The American Psychoanalyst*, *45*(4), 13–14, 16.

Kris, E. (1956). On Some Vicissitudes of Insight in Psycho-Analysis 1. *Int. J. Psycho-Anal.*, *37*, 445–455.

Kuhn, T. (1962). *The Structure of Scientific Revolutions*. Chicago, IL: University of Chicago Press.

Leslie, A. M., & Thaiss, L. (1992). Domain specificity in conceptual development: Neuropsychological evidence from autism. *Cognition*, *43*(3), 225–251. doi:10.1016/0010-0277(92)90013-8.

Levin, F. M. (2000). Learning, Development, and Psychopathology: Applying Chaos Theory to Psychoanalysis. *Ann. Psychoanal.*, *28*, 85–104.

Levine, H. B. (2012). The Colourless Canvas: Representation, Therapeutic Action and the Creation of Mind. *Int. J. Psycho-Anal.*, *93*, 607–629.

Lewis, J. D. (2012). Towards a Unified Theory of Trauma and Its Consequences. *Int. J. Appl. Psychoanal. Stud.*, *9*, 298–317.

Loewald, H. W. (1988). Termination Analyzable and Unanalyzable. *Psychoanal. St. Child*, *43*, 155–166.

Lotterman, M. (2011). Psychotherapy Can Benefit Schizophrenic Patients. *The American Psychoanalyst*, *45*(4), 12, 15–16.

Mahler, M. S., Pine, F., & Bergman, A. (1975). *The psychological birth of the human infant: Symbiosis and individuation*. New York: Basic Books.

Marcus, E. (2012). Creativity in Psychosis. *The American Psychoanalyst*, *46*(2), 19.

Matthis, I. (2000). Sketch for a Metapsychology of Affect. *Int. J. Psycho-Anal.*, *81*, 215–227.

Mayes, L. C. (2001). The Twin Poles of Order and Chaos: Development as a Dynamic, Self-ordering System. *Psychoanal. St. Child*, *56*, 137–170.

Miller, J. M. (2002). Anna Freud: A view of development, disturbance, and therapeutic techniques: Rose Edgcumbe. London/Philadelphia, PA: Routledge, 2000. *Psychoanalytic Quarterly*, *71*(1), 139–142.

Moran, M. G. (1991). Chaos Theory and Psychoanalysis:—The Fluidic Nature of the Mind. *Int. R. Psycho-Anal.*, *18*, 211–221.

Novak, B. J. (2004). From Chaos to Developmental Growth: Working through Trauma to Achieve Adolescence in the Analysis of an Adopted Russian Orphan. *Psychoanal. St. Child*, *59*, 74–99.

Palombo, S. R. (1999). *The Emergent Ego: Complexity and Coevolution in the Psychoanalytic Process*. Madison, CT: International University Press.

Parens, H. (2011). *Parenting for Emotional Growth: A Textbook, Workshops, and Curriculum for Students in Grades K-12*. Philadelphia: Jefferson Medical College.

Piers, C., Muller, J., & Brent, J. (Eds.). (2007). *Self-Organizing Complexity in Psychological Systems*. Lanham, MD: Jason Aronson.

Poincaré, H. (1890). Sur le probléme des trois corps et les équations de la dynamique. *Acta Mathematica*, *13*(1), A3–A270. doi:10.1007/BF02392506

Quinodoz, J. (1997). Transitions in Psychic Structures in the Light of Deterministic Chaos Theory. *Int. J. Psycho-Anal.*, *78*, 699–718.

Ramis, H. (1993). *Groundhog Day*. Columbia Pictures. Retrieved from http://en.wikipedia.org/w/index.php?title=Groundhog_Day_(film)&oldid=564089253.

Reich, W. (1933). *Character Analysis*. New York, NY: Macmillan.

Samenow, J. (2012, November 1). The National Hurricane Center's strikingly accurate forecast for Sandy. *The Washington Post - Blogs*. Retrieved from http://www.washingtonpost.com/blogs/capital-weather-gang/post/the-national-hurricane-centers-striking-forecast-for-super-storm-sandy/2012/11/01/e2633b5e-2427-11e2-ac85-e669876c6a24_blog.html.

Schachtel, E. (1959). *Metamorphosis*. New York, NY: Basic Books, Inc.

Scott Janssen, L. (2012). Community Mental Health, Psychosis, and Psychodynamics: The Perfect Combination? *The American Psychoanalyst*, *46*(1), 23–24.

Searles, H. F. (1961). Anxiety Concerning Change, as Seen in the Psychotherapy of Schizophrenic Patients—with Particular Reference to the Sense of Personal Identity. *Int. J. Psycho-Anal.*, *42*, 74–85.

Searles, H. F. (1976). Psychoanalytic Therapy with Schizophrenic Patients in a Private-Practice Context. *Contemp. Psychoanal.*, *12*, 387–406.

Sherkow, S. P. (2004). Further Reflections on the "Watched" Play State and the Role of "Watched Play" in Analytic Work. *Psychoanal. St. Child*, *59*, 55–73.

Slevin, M., & Marcus, E. (2011). Introduction. *The American Psychoanalyst*, *45*(4), 1.

Spitz, R. A. (1945). Diacritic and Coenesthetic Organizations: The Psychiatric Significance of a Functional Division of the Nervous System into a Sensory and Emotive Part. *Psychoanal. Rev.*, *32*, 146–162.

Spitz, R. A., & Cobliner, W. G. (1965). *The first year of life: A psychoanalytic study of normal and deviant development of object relations*. New York: International Universities Press.

Spruiell, V. (1993). Deterministic Chaos and the Sciences of Complexity: Psychoanalysis in the Midst of a General Scientific Revolution. *J. Amer. Psychoanal. Assn.*, *41*, 3–44.

Stern, D. B. (1983). Unformulated Experience: From Familiar Chaos to Creative Disorder 1. *Contemp. Psychoanal.*, *19*, 71–99.

Stone, M. (2012). Establishing Empathy by Analyzing Psychosis. *The American Psychoanalyst*, *46*(1), 18–19.

Sugarman, A. (2003). Dimensions of the Child Analyst's Role as a Developmental Object: Affect Regulation and Limit Setting. *Psychoanal. St. Child*, *58*, 189–213.

Tyson, P. (2005). Affects, Agency, and Self-Regulation: Complexity Theory in the Treatment of Children with Anxiety and Disruptive Behavior Disorders. *J. Amer. Psychoanal. Assn.*, *53*, 159–187.

Varela, F., Thompson, E., & Rosch, E. (1991). *The Embodied Mind*. Cambridge, MA: MIT Press.

Verhulst, F. (1999). Psychoanalysis and chaos theory. *Int. J. Psycho-Anal.*, *80*, 623–625.

Verhulst, F. (1994). Metaphors for psychoanalysis. *Nonlinear Science Today*, *4*, 1–6.

Wallace, A. F. (1970). *Culture and Personality* (2nd ed.). New York, NY: Random House.

Weiss, P. (1949). The Biological Basis of Adaptation. In J. Romano (Ed.), *Adaptation*. Ithaca, NY: Cornell University Press.

Winnicott, D. W. (1960). The Theory of the Parent-Infant Relationship 1. *Int. J. Psycho-Anal.*, *41*, 585–595.

Winnicott, D. W. (1971). Mirror-role of mother and family in child development. In *Playing and Reality* (pp. 111–118). Middlesex: Penguin.

Index

About the Authors

Theodore Fallon, MD, MPH, is an internist and epidemiologist, and has twenty-five years of experience as a child and adult psychiatrist and psychoanalyst. He is the director of the Child and Adolescent Psychoanalytic Training Program at the Psychoanalytic Center of Philadelphia. He is also clinical associate professor at Drexel University College of Medicine.

Susan P. Sherkow, MD, is a training and supervising analyst at the Berkshire Psychoanalytic Institute and Society and an instructor and supervising analyst at the New York Psychoanalytic Institute and Society. She has forty years of experience working with children on the autism spectrum.